A Confederacy of Evil

Cardinal Newman on the End Times

With an Introductory Essay
by the late Fr. Vincent P. Miceli, S.J.

A Confederacy of Evil

Cardinal Newman on the End Times

With an Introductory Essay
by the late Fr. Vincent P. Miceli, S.J.

Roman Catholic Books
P. O. Box 2286 • Fort Collins, CO 80522
BooksforCatholics.com

Contents

Publisher's Preface.. vii

Introduction... ix

Chapter I: The Times of Antichrist......................................1

Chapter II: The Religion of Antichrist 23

Chapter III: The City of Antichrist 41

Chapter IV: The Persecution of Antichrist........................61

Publisher's Preface

The "Advent Sermons" of Blessed John Henry (Cardinal) Newman, in which the masterful patristics scholar and pastor of souls discourses on the Antichrist and the End Times, applying the signs to our own era, are among his most important.

The great Oratorian founder was stricken by the alarming portents, mostly intellectual in nature in his day, well before the mass murders sponsored by three atheists, Hitler, Stalin and Mao. The two great wars of the 20th century were well ahead of him. Yet he seemed to sense what lay shortly ahead.

What the last century produced, it is safe to say, would only have eroded Newman's remaining reserve.

Indeed, since the moral revolution in the mid-1960s, during which attitudes of hatred toward established Christian norms were dramatically advanced, a setting of wickedness has become the backdrop of our lives in the West. It's perhaps sufficient to explain what has befallen us to younger generations to note that even mildly crude language and the word "sex" was once banned from American TV—now the arbiter of what is normal in the eyes of the world—and pornographers and sodomites were once shamed rather than celebrated by society.

In Europe and the Americas, where easy acceptance of abortion was considered unthinkable, hundreds of millions of unborn have been wiped out since the 1960s—following the revolution in established law which is always a pre-requisite for high crimes against God and man.

Newman, in the words of Malcolm Muggeridge, who was born a decade after the cardinal died, "foresaw with unique clarity how in our time" the dire prophecies of Sacred Scripture might be coming to pass. But Newman also saw that "God never leaves us in total darkness."

The sobering pages that follow, along with an introduction by the late Jesuit preacher and teacher, Fr. Vincent Miceli, clearly focus the reader's attention on the central tragedy of contemporary life—Christ has been rejected by society, while the guardians of the Church seem to have adjusted a little too easily to leading foes of the Church, many of them Catholic, in the U.S. leadership realm.

The flock remains confused, not to say in near-total route.

Introduction

John Henry Newman is beyond doubt one of the greatest minds and noblest persons of the nineteenth century. In him we have a rare, yet winsome, combination of learning, originality, sound judgement, profundity and holiness. A divine philosopher, man of letters, and pastor of souls, Newman was the leader of the Oxford Tractarian Movement and the most illustrious of English converts to the Catholic Church. His long, yet meteoric, career spanned the years 1801 to 1890.

Having loved and immersed himself in the works of the early Fathers of the Church, Newman became in his own right such a master of Catholic philosophy, theology, morals and Scripture that he can truly be called a nineteenth-century Father of the Church. Even in his own day he accomplished lasting work. He resuscitated the Fathers, brought into relief the sacramental system, paved the way for an astonishing revival of the long-forgotten ritual, and gave the clergy a new hold upon thousands at the moment when, in England, Erastian principles—theories of secular supremacy in religious affairs—were on the eve of triumph. Throughout his life the motto of Oxford remained his continual inspiration: *Dominus illuminatio mea*: The Lord is my light. And two of the most important rules that guided his conduct towards God and his fellowmen were: "Holiness rather than peace," and "Growth the only evidence of life." His greatness consisted in the harmony of his genius of the first rank with a deep spiritual temper, in a personality no less winning than sensitive. Indeed, among the literary stars of his time, Newman was distinguished by the pure Christian radiance shining in his life and writings. He is the one Englishman of that era who upheld the ancient Creed with a knowledge and fervor that only the early Fathers possessed. In the exposition of that creed he developed and used a Shakespearean force of style and a zeal worthy of the saints. It is this unique combination that raised him above the lay preacher *de vanitate mundi* like Thackeray and which gave him a place apart from Tennyson and Browning. Newman is the great Christian and Catholic apologist, the Augustinian type of controversialist in an epoch of Agnosticism amid the forces of evolution.

On a voyage to North Africa, Italy, Western Greece and Sicily (December 1832-July 1833), Newman the Anglican stopped in Rome and for the rest if his life the city laid a spell of religion upon him which was never to be diminished. At Leonforte in Sicily he took seriously ill with a fever and was nursed back from the jaws of death by a peasant. Yet during his illness Newman was convinced that he would not die, that God was calling him to some religious high mission. He cried out: "I shall not die; I have not sinned against the light." On his way home, while his ship was becalmed in the straits of Bonifacio, Newman sought God's guidance toward the truth and his Church in his famous poem-prayer, "Lead, Kindly Light," deservedly treasured today by all nations, especially English-speaking peoples.

Back in England, Newman began "Tracts for the Times," as he tells us with a smile, "out of my own head." He was trying to justify his own religious apostolate in the Anglican Church which he held to be one branch, along with the corrupted Catholic Church and the Greek Church of the true Church. He held that these three were accidental ritual variations of the one true Christian society. In 1841 his "Tract 90" tried to reconcile the Anglican Thirty-Nine Articles with the Council of Trent, an impossible undertaking even for the genius of Newman. During the previous eight years of writing the tracts, Newman took his motto from the *Iliad*: "They (the enemies) shall know the difference now." During these years he won victory after victory only to be defeated finally by his own weapon when "Tract 90" antagonized the Anglican hierarchy. Censored severely, he retired to his tent in Littlemore, a broken champion in 1841. But in 1845, after four years of silence, study, prayer, and penance, Newman was received into the Catholic Church on October 8, 1845 by Father Demenico Barbieri—today Blessed Barbieri—a Passionist mystic who had long sacrificed himself as a missionary for the conversion of England

Even in his Anglican days Newman was a great preacher. But he preached without eloquence or gesture of popular gifts. His genius was thrilling earnestness and a knowledge of human nature seldom equalled. When published it was said his sermons "beat all other sermons on the market as Scott's tales beat all other stories." Their chastened style, fertility of illustration and sharp energy have lost nothing by age. In tone they are severe and often melancholy, as if the utterances of an isolated prophet crying in the wilderness. His eight volumes of *"Parochial and Plain Sermons"* are admirable in their profound interpretation of Scripture and, though written in his non-Catholic period, have very little in them to which Catholics can object. His Catholic *"Sermons to Mixed Congregations"* exceed in vigor and irony all other sermons ever published by him. For once he became a Catholic, his genius bloomed out with a force and freedom it never displayed in Anglican communion. Listen to the words of R.H. Hutton on Newman the Catholic convert: "In irony, in humor, in eloquence, in imaginative force, the writings of the later and, as we may call it, the emancipated portion of his career far surpass the writings of his theological apprenticeship."

Because of Newman's Tracts, patristic studies became the order of the day. His first volume, *The Arians of the Fourth Century*, dealt with creeds and sects of that heresy. His *Apologia Pro Vita Sua* gives us the key to his mental development and his judgement on the great religious revival known as the Oxford Movement. It also devastated Charles Kingsley's accusation against the Catholic Church. "Truth," wrote Kingsley, "for its own sake has never been a virtue with the Roman clergy. Father Newman informs us that it need not, and on the whole ought not, to be; that cunning is the weapon which heaven is given to the saints wherewith to withstand the brute male force of the wicked world which marries and is given in marriage." In his brilliant annihilation of this calumny, Newman won great admiration for himself and Catholic faith. We can only mention here some of Newman's other important woks. An *Essay on the Development of Christian Doctrine* aimed at harmonizing the apparent variations in dogma with the Catholic Church's claim to be the same Church that goes back to the Apostles in an unbroken living tradition. Newman's theory of the organic development of dogma in the crucible of historical trials is a magnificent contribution to the understanding of the economy of salvation as God reveals its secrets in unrolling history. His *Idea of a University* exhibits a range of thought, an urbanity of style, a pregnant wit, and an understanding of the nature of the Catholic education that is brilliant and unrivaled. It is still the best exposition and defense of Catholic educational theories in any language. But Newman is also a poet and playwright. *His Dream of Gerontius* far excels the meditative verse of modern bards by its felicitous shadowing forth in symbols and dramatic scenes of the world beyond this vale of tears.

Besides being a master of thought and style, Newman was a mystic and prophet who enjoyed the deepest insight into the future of the Church. It is under this aspect of his genius that we will consider his treatment of the Antichrist. For Newman always looked beyond the immediate future in his love and concern for the Church. In a lecture given at Dublin on "A From of Infidelity of the Day," he seems to have anticipated the great apostasy from the Church via the heretical road of Modernism and neo-Modernism. He called this heresy "the religion of reason," and condemned it as the ruin of all revealed truth of all supernatural fate. He foresaw the total loss of the Church's temporal power; he predicted the positive role of the faithful in the infallible teaching of the Magisterium. To his own generation he became a Jeremiah, decrying the abandonment of the fate by many in the Church and the disease of religious liberalism within its bosom.

Despondency was his prevailing mood and, though he was long under a cloud of suspicion for heresey both in and outside the Church, Newman never despaired. He clearly, courageously expounded, defended and advanced the Catholic faith to all who would listen. Though gracious and even tenderhearted, Newman's peculiar temper included deep reserve. He had not in his composition, as he says, "a grain of conviviality." He was always the Oxford Scholar, no democrat, suspicious of popular movements, but keenly interested in political studies and affairs as bearing on the fortunes of the Church. Yet his motto as a Cardinal, *"Cor ad cor loquitur,"* "Heart speaks to heart," reveals that this great Catholic genius was one in mind and heart with the most illustrious of all the Fathers, St. Augustine who had written: "The final word is not with thought, nor with reason, nor with the head, but with love, with the will, with the heart." Newman expressed his thought on the Antichrist in four famous Advent sermons on that subject: The Times of Antichrist; The Religion of Antichrist; The City of Antichrist; The Persecution of Antichrist.

Chapter I: *The Times of the Antichrist*

Newman consults Holy Scripture, the Fathers of the Church and great historical figures in order to describe events which will usher in the times of the Antichrist. The day of the Antichrist will not come until there is a great falling away from God, Christ and the Church. This frightful apostasy and the advent of the man of sin shall precede Christ's final coming. Yet the coming of the Antichrist shall be prepared by "false prophets," "false Christ's," "the showing of signs and wonders," "iniquity abounding," and "love waxing cold" in the whole world. These signs will tell us that the day of the Lord is near, event at the doors, for the Antichrist comes immediately before the Second Coming of Christ. Two other great signs will herald the imminent coming of the Antichrist. There will be worldwide confusion and trouble, "great tribulation, such as was not from the beginning of the world until this time, and this Gospel shall be preached in all the world for a witness unto all nations; and then shall come the end." But what is the meaning of the words "the mystery of iniquity is already at work"? According to Newman, they mean that in all times, even in St. Paul's day, there are shadows, forebodings, earnests, and evil elements preparing for the day in which wickedness will arrive in all its fullness. Just as there have always been types of Christ preceding and preparing the way for the coming of Christ, so the shadows of the Antichrist will precede him. Even the days of the Apostles typified the last days; there were false Christ's, national then, and international upheavals. Then the true Christ came in judgement to destroy the unfaithful among the Jews. "In truth," Newman writes, "every event in the world is a type of those that follow, history proceeding forward as a circle ever enlarging.... For every age presents its own picture of those future events which alone are the real fulfillment of the prophecy which stands at the head of them all."

We have seen that St. Paul told the Thessalonians that the Antichrist could not come in their era because something or someone was restraining his coming. What was this restraining power that delayed the manifestation of the enemy of truth? "Now you know what restrains him that they may be revealed in his proper time." Who, or what is this restraining power? According to Newman, it is generally admitted to be the Roman Empire. Just as Rome succeeded Greece in Daniel's vision, so the Antichrist succeeds Rome and Christ the Savior succeeds the Antichrist. Newman argues that the Antichrist has not yet come because the entire Roman Empire has not yet been thoroughly vanquished, has not yet disappeared from the face of the earth. Newman thought that important vestiges of the Roman Empire survived into the nineteenth century. For the ten horns or kingdoms, of which Daniel speaks, and into which the Roman Empire will be divided, still exist. Until they are thoroughly removed the Antichrist will not come. Out of the little horn will eventually arise the Antichrist, "with the eyes of a man and a mouth speaking great things."

The Antichrist will embody the spirit of infidelity par excellence. Newman claimed that this malignant spirit, this fierce and lawless principle, was at work even in his own day. This spirit of ambition, the mother of all heresy, schism, sedition, revolution and war was being held back by the framework of society and government that Newman's time inherited, a representative of Roman power, a still functioning legacy of the Roman Empire to the modern world.

Newman asks whether the Antichrist will be one man, an individual, or a power or a kingdom? The Holy Scripture, the living tradition of the Church and the consensus of the Fathers led him to conclude that the Antichrist will be one man, a person. For he is called in Scripture "the man of sin," "the son of perdition," "the adversary and rival of all that is called God or worshipped," "the one who sits as God in the temple of God, proclaiming himself to be god." He is the wicked one "whom the Lord shall consume with the spirit of His mouth and shall destroy with the brightness of His coming....Whose coming is after the working of Satan with all power and signs and lying wonders." Then too, Daniel speaks of the Antichrist "subduing three kings, speaking words against the Most High, thinking to change times and laws, ruling for a time and times and the dividing of time." Again: "The judgement shall sit and they shall take away his dominion, to consume and destroy it unto the end." Daniel also relates the duplicity whereby he comes to power.

In his estate shall stand up a vile person, to whom they shall not give the honor of the kingdom; but he shall come in peaceably, and obtain the kingdom by flatteries....And such as do wickedly against the covenant shall be corrupt by flatteries; but the people that do know their God shall be strong and do exploits....And the king shall do according to his will; and he shall exalt himself, and magnify himself above every god, and shall speak marvelous things against the God of gods, prosper till the indignation be accomplished.... Neither shall he regard the God of his fathers, nor the desire of women, nor regard any god; for he shall magnify himself above all. But in his estate shall he honor the God of forces, and a God whom his fathers knew not shall he honor with gold and silver, and with precious stones and pleasant things

St. John says of this wicked person:

There was given him a mouth speaking great things and blasphemies; and power was given unto him to continue forty and two months and he opened his mouth in blasphemy against God, to blaspheme His name and His tabernacle and them that dwell in heaven. And it was given him to make war with the saints, and to overcome them; and power was given him over all kindreds and tongues and nations. And all that dwell upon the earth shall worship him whose names are not written in the book of life of the lamb slain from the foundation of the world.

Newman also presents an argument from probability to persuade his reader that the Antichrist will be an individual person. He chooses three remarkable shadows, among many that could be selected, that answer closely to the descriptions of what the Antichrist will be and do when he comes. For if the types and forerunners of the Antichrist are famous historical persons, then the Antichrist will have to be even more so a world-famous person. From the shadows of the Antichrist we can learn much about the substantial Antichrist.

Prior to the advent of Christ, perhaps the most remarkable shadow of the coming fulfillment of evil in the Antichrist was the heathen, King Antiochus, of whom we read in the book of Maccabees. Daniel also has much to say about this shadow, his terms and descriptions clearly pointing to King Antiochus and simultaneously to the Antichrist. These terms imply that Antiochus was a type of that monster who will ravage the Church at the end of time.

Antiochus was a savage persecutor of the Jews. Some Jewish apostates, seeking the power and pleasures of this world, made a covenant with him. They made themselves uncircumcised, forsook the holy covenant with God, joined the heathen and sold themselves to perform all manner of mischief. When Antiochus had conquered Egypt, he advanced against Israel and Jerusalem. He sacked the city, profaned the temple, removed the golden altar, the candlestick of light, all the sacred vessels, the vials, the censers of gold, the veils, the crowns, the golden ornaments; he pulled down every sacred symbol. Claiming to be God, he massacred the people, set fire to Jerusalem, and "pulled down the houses and walls thereof on every side." Then he rebuilt the city of David; he settled the sinful nation in the city, wicked men and women, and fortified it. Then King Antiochus assimilated the Jews under his heathen laws, demanding that they abandon the law of God under penalty of death. The Jews accepted the religion of a pagan idolatry, sacrificed to false gods and profaned the sabbath. The king forced other impieties upon the Jews. Those who remained faithful to their covenant and sabbaths, he put to death. But the majority polluted the sanctuary, visited the altars and groves of idols, and sacrificed swine's flesh and unclean beasts. Finally, Antiochus set up a great idol or, in the words of history, "the Abomination of Desolation" upon the altar, and built idol altars throughout the cities of Judah. When he had torn the books of the law into shreds,he consigned them to the fire. "Here," says Newman, "we have presented to us some of the lineaments of the Antichrist who will be such and worse than such, as Antiochus."

Another such shadow was the Emperor Julian the Apostate. He lived between 331-363 A.D. His example also indicates that the Antichrist will be one person, not a kingdom or power. Julian fell away from the Catholic faith, mounted a persecution of Christians and attempted to reestablish pagan idolatry as the religion of the empire. He proudly undertook to rebuild the temple of Jerusalem, having gathered all the men and materials to do so. But trouble in the eastern part of his empire called him to the front to quell an uprising. In the ensuing battle Julian was killed and his plans to crush the Church were totally frustrated. Newman presents the false prophet Muhammad as a third historical shadow of the Antichrist. This shadow began his imposture about 600 years after Christ and his armies tore at the soul and body of Christ in the fierce religious wars they waged against the Church. Finally Newman refers indirectly to the godless leaders of the French Revolution who attacked the Church fiercely, laicized France and spread revolt against God and His Church throughout Europe and the world. In every case of a forerunner of the Antichrist, Newman demonstrates how the apostasy of the people from the true God prepared the coming of these heralds and types of the Antichrist and led to the wholesale slaughter of a religious society. First the people of God in large numbers discarded their sacred religion and then the enemy was allowed to come in. The great apostasy is always the harbinger of the shadows and substance of the Antichrist. The Jews first abandoned God, then came Antiochus; Christians first fell away into Arianism, then arose Julian the Apostate and the persecution; the heresies of Nestorianism and Eutychianism destroyed the faith of millions, then came Muhammad. The agnosticism and atheism of the Enlightenment paved the way for the Reign of Terror under Robespierre and the Jacobins.

Newman then reflects on his own times to see if there are growing signs of the coming of the Antichrist. "Is the enemy of Christ and his Church to arise in our times from a certain special falling away from God?" Without answering Yes or No, Newman describes the conditions of this time as favorable to an early arrival of the Antichrist. There are evidences to convince us that we are entering the Age of

Apostasy. For apostasy is being formed, gathering forces, gaining ground on the Church every day. Everywhere in the world, but quite visibly and formidably in the most peaceful, civilized nations, we are witnessing a supreme effort to govern men and dominate the world without religion. It is a widely accepted and spreading dogma that nations should have nothing to do with religion, that religion is merely a private matter, an affair of one's own conscience. In effect it is widely accepted that Truth is neither a personal nor a social need and, therefore, society ought to allow Truth to fade from the face of the earth. It is considered futile social action to continue to advance a system of Truth and absurd to attempt to hand it on further developed organically to our posterity. In almost every country there is a united, powerful movement to crush the Church, to strip her of power and place. Everywhere we discover a feverish, litigious endeavor to get rid of religion in public activities—in schools, in mass media, in social transactions, in political affairs. Societies are said to be built on the principle of Utility, not on the principle of Truth. Experience, not Truth or Justice, is accepted as the end or rule of state activities, enactments of law included. Numbers not Truth is the final ground for maintaining this or that creed, morality or law, it being generally believed that the many are always in the right, the few in the wrong. Even the Bible is given so many meanings over and against its obvious one that it is reduced to having no meaning at all, to being at best a pleasant myth, at worst a dead letter. In the end religion is denied any objective, historical reality such as is displayed in written dogmas, ordinances and sacraments. Religion is rather confined to each person's inner feelings, experiences and psychological reactions. Thus cast into the dark world of variable, evanescent, volatile feelings, religion is discredited in the minds of many when, it is not already destroyed.

"Surely," continues Newman, "there is at this day a confederacy of evil, marshaling its hosts from all parts of the world, organizing itself, taking its measures, enclosing the Church of Christ as in a net, and preparing the way for general apostasy from it....This Apostasy and all its tokens and instruments are of the evil one and savior of death." How does the Evil One bring about the apostasy? "He offers baits to tempt men: he promises liberty, equality, trade and wealth, remission of taxes, reforms. He tempts men to rail against their rulers and superiors in imitation of his own revolution. He promises illumination, knowledge, science, philosophy, enlargement of mind. He scoffs at times gone by, at sacred traditions, at every institution which reveres them. He bids man mount aloft, to become a god. He laughs and jokes with men, gets intimate with them, takes their hands, gets his fingers between theirs, grasps them and then they are his." Newman was convinced that the shadows of the Antichrist in his day, some one hundred years or so ago, were thickening and lengthening as the age of darkness approached.

Chapter II: *The Religion of the Antichrist*

Newman takes directly from St. John the Evangelist the characteristic that will reveal the Antichrist when he comes. He will openly deny Our Lord Jesus Christ to be the Son of God come in the flesh from heaven. In fact, the denial of Christ can be called the spirit of the Antichrist; those who deny Christ can be said to have the spirit of the Antichrist; to be like the Antichrist, to be themselves antichrists, albeit on a smaller scale. "Who is a liar," asks St. John, "but he who denies that Jesus is the Christ?"

St. Paul and St. John speak of the same enemy of the Church. This is discovered from the similarity of their descriptions. Both claim that the spirit of the Antichrist was already at work in their day. "That spirit of the Antichrist," says St. John, "is now already in the world." "The mystery of iniquity is already at work," says St. Paul. Both describe the enemy as being scarred with the same special sin—open infidelity. St. John writes: "He is the Antichrist who denies the Father and the Son." St. Paul identifies him in like manner as "the adversary and rival of all that is called God, setting forth himself as if he were God." In every case we find the same blasphemous denial of God and religion. And St. Paul scores the final blasphemy: "He will oppose all existing religion, true or false, all that is called God or worshipped."

The prophet Daniel decries the same reckless impiety in

the Antichrist:

"The king shall do according to his will; and he shall exalt himself and magnify himself above every god, and shall speak marvelous things against the God of Gods, and shall prosper until the indignation be accomplished....Neither shall he regard the God of his fathers, nor the desire of women (that is, as it would appear, the Messiah, to be his mother being the especial privilege and object of hope among the Jewish women), nor regard any god—for he shall magnify himself above all."

Christ's words to the high priests plotting His death also give a deeply prophetic allusion to the blasphemous designs of the Antichrist. "I am come in My Father's name, and you do not receive Me; if another shall come in his own name, him you will receive." This, according to the Fathers, is a prophetic allusion to the Antichrist whom the Jews will mistake for the Christ. He comes in his own name, not from God, as even the Son of God came, who, if any, might have come with the power of his essential divinity.

Then there are the Scripture passages which speak generally of the impieties of the last age of the world, impieties which will usher in and be completed in the culmination of evil in the Antichrist.

....Many shall be purified and made white and tried. But the wicked shall do wickedly; and none of the wicked shall understand....in the last days perilous times shall come, for men shall be lovers of their own selves, covetous, boasters, proud, blasphemers, disobedient to parents, unthankful, unholy, without natural affection, truce-breakers, false accusers, incontinent, fierce, despisers of those that are good, traitors, heady, high-minded, lovers of pleasures more than lovers of God, having a form of godliness but denying the power thereof; scoffers walking after their own lusts, and saying, Where is the promise of His coming?; despising government, presumptuous...self-willed, not afraid to speak evil of dignities...promising men liberty, while themselves the servants of corruption.

Newman than expounds on why the Antichrist is to be connected with the Jewish race. The ANtichrist will come saying: "I am Christ." But the Jews, having rejected the true Christ, will now have to undergo the judicial punishment imposed upon themselves by their stubborn blindness to the light of Christ. They will be taken in by the false Christ. For the Antichrist will be the consummate, the complete deceiver, "whose coming," says St. Paul:

is...with all the wicked deception to those who are perishing because they have not received the love of truth, that they might be saved. Therefore, God sends them a misleading influence that they may believe falsehood, that all may be judged who have not believed in the truth, but took pleasure in wickedness.

Since the Antichrist will pose as the Messiah, it has been universally accepted by the Christian tradition that he would be of the Jewish race and observe the Jewish rites. Moreover, according to St. Paul, the Antichrist will "sit in the Temple of God,"—the Jewish Temple—according to the Fathers. Our Lord's own words support this prediction when he speaks of "the abomination of desolation" (an expression denoting the Antichrist in his full wickedness), "standing in the holy place." Then, too, St. John describes the Antichrist's persecution of the two witnesses of Christ, Elias and Enoch, as taking place in Jerusalem. "Their dead bodies shall lie in the street of the great city, which is spiritually called Sodom and Egypt, where also Our Lord was crucified."

Newman then asks a most important question. Will the Antichrist profess any sort of religion? Scripture tells us that he will worship neither true nor false God. For the Antichrist is "to exalt himself over all that is called God or worshipped." He will set himself forcefully against idols and idolatry. Yet Daniel writes:"In his estate shall he honor the God of force, and a God whom his fathers knew not shall he honor with gold and silver, and with precious stones and pleasant things. Thus shall he do in the most strong holds with a strange god, whom he shall acknowledge and increase with glory."

The meaning of the words "God of force" and "a strange God" is, according to Newman, "quite hidden from us and probably will be so till the event." Yet some sort of false worship is certainly predicted as the mark of the Antichrist, despite the fact that Daniel asserts that "he shall set himself against all idols," as well as against the true God. This apparent contradiction should not surprise the faithful. For it is generally known to the saints that infidelity leads to superstition and blasphemers are really cowards. Take the example of Catholic France, which during the French Revolution became a laicized, atheistic state. Atheism was absolutely professed as the State religion. In spite of this, a certain strange worship was set up. The state leaders forced a Catholic Archbishop to come forward and declare publicly that there was no God. They closed the churches, and seized and desecrated the gold and silver vessels from the sanctuaries. They formed mock processions of men clad in priestly garments and singing profane hymns. They annulled the divine ordinance of marriage, reducing it to a mere civil contract. They exalted the very negation of religion, their living blasphemy into a kind of god, calling it Liberty. And they literally worshipped it as a divinity. Rejecting Christ as an impostor, they decreed in the public assembly of the nation the adoration of Liberty and Equality as divinities. And they appointed festivals in honor of Reason, the Country, the Constitution and the Virtues. They determined that tutelary gods, even dead men, were to be canonized, and consecrated and worshipped; and they enrolled in the lists of these some of the most notorious infidels and profligates. This infatuated, godless people tried to reinstate the old Roman democratic worship, as if to prove that Rome, the fourth monster of the Prophet's vision, was not dead. They even raised a statue to Ceres, a Roman divinity, and appointed a festival in her honor. This new pagan religion of atheistic France demonstrated that the evil spirit of old Rome was still active in the world, though its name was almost extinct. In the end these apostates bowed down to the goddess of Reason in the person of a nude prostitute whom they placed on the high altar of Notre Dame cathedral in Paris.

In summarizing the religion of the Antichrist, Newman stresses these conclusions of the Fathers of the Church. 1) The Antichrist will come out of the Roman Empire, upon its division into ten kingdoms. 2) The Antichrist will come up suddenly out of it upon these ten, subdue three of them, and finally all of them. 3) The Antichrist will then blaspheme, puffed up with power and glory, and use great words against the Most High. 4) After remaining torpid for centuries, the Roman monster will awake at the end of the world and be restored in all its laws and forms. 5) The system of Augustus, founder of the Roman Empire, will be adopted and established by the Antichrist to his own aggrandizement and glory. 6) This is the fourth monster, whose head was wounded and healed—the empire was destroyed and divided into ten. 7) This time the Antichrist, a man of power and wonderful resources, will heal and restore this monster so that it will vigorously fight once again against the camp of the saints. 8) The name of the Antichrist is the very number 666, which will reveal him as "the Abomination of Desolation." But the true meaning of his name will remain a mystery until the historical event of the Antichrist's arrival takes place.

In short, the Antichrist will be an open blasphemer, opposed to all worship true or false. He will be a persecutor of the Church, but a patron to all the Jews, a restorer of their worship. He will be the author of a novel kind of worship. He will appear suddenly from the end of the Roman empire, which was once and now sleeps. He will knit that Roman empire again into one, engraft his Judaism and new Paganism onto the old discipline of Caesar Augustus, thereby earning for himself the title of Roman king, and the divine honors of an emperor. He will rule for three and one-half years and then pass away suddenly as he appeared.

Chapter III: *The City of the Antichrist*

The intimate connection of the city of Rome with the exploits and reign of the Antichrist leads Newman to speculate that Rome may turn out to be the city of the Antichrist in the last times. Even the Fathers of the Church leaned heavily toward this interpretation. The influence of the Roman Empire permeates the Gospels, the Acts of the Apostles, the Epistles, especially of Paul and the Apocalypse. Christ was born, lived, suffered and died under the Romans.

St. Paul, a Roman citizen, was at times protected, at times persecuted and finally executed by Roman power. The same is true, though to a lesser degree, with the other Apostles. The great city which ruled over the kings of the earth first severely persecuted and finally promulgated Christianity.

In chapter seventeen of the Apocalypse, St. John describes the great city of Rome under the image of a woman: she is cruel, profligate, impious. She is arrayed in worldly splendor and costliness, in purple and scarlet, in gold and precious stones and pearls. She sheds and drinks the blood of the saints, becomes drunk on it. She is called "Babylon the Great," to signify her power, wealth, profanity, pride, sensuality and persecuting spirit. When St. John was writing his Apocalypse, the city of Rome was the historical embodiment of the above description. Newman tells us:

"There never was a more ambitious, haughty, hardhearted and worldly people than the Romans; never any, for none else had ever the opportunity, which so persecuted the Church. Christians suffered ten persecutions at their hands—and very horrible ones, extending over 250 years."

St. John represented this city of sin as an abandoned woman, seated on a "scarlet-colored monster, full of names of blasphemy, having seven heads and ten horns." This image drives us back to Daniel's prophetic description in which the four great empires of the world are shadowed under the figure of four beasts—a lion, a bear, a leopard and a nameless monster, this last different from the rest, "dreadful and terrible and strong exceedingly." This is surely the same beast which St. John saw; the ten horns identify it. Now this fourth beast in Daniel's vision is the Roman empire: "the beast," therefore on which woman sits is also the Roman empire. History bears out this interpretation, for Rome, the mistress of the world, might well be said to have sat upon, and been carried about triumphantly on that world which she had subdued and made her creature. Daniel explains the ten horns of the Beast to be "ten Kings that shall arise" out of this empire. St. John agrees, saying: "The ten horns which you saw are the ten kings, which have received no kingdom as yet, but receive power as kings one hour with the beast." Then, too, in an earlier vision Daniel speaks of the empire as destined to be "divided," as "partly strong and partly broken." Moreover, this empire, the beast of burden of the woman, was at length to rise against her and devour her; it would do this in the time of its divided existence. "The ten horns which you saw upon the beast, these shall hate her, and shall make her desolate and naked, and shall eat her flesh and burn her with fire." Such was to be the end of the great city of iniquity. Lastly, three of the kings, maybe all of them, are said to be subdued or won over by the Antichrist, who is to come up suddenly while they are in power. Thus does Daniel prophesy the event:

"Another shall rise after them, and he shall be diverse from the first, and he shall subdue three kings, and shall speak great words against the Most High, and shall wear out the saints of the Most High, and think to change times and laws; and they shall be given into his hands until a time, times and a dividing of time."

This power which rises up against the kings is the Antichrist. And here we should observe how Rome and the Antichrist are further related to each other in the prophecy.

Rome is to fall before the Antichrist rises. For the ten kings are to destroy Rome; then the Antichrist appears to supersede the ten kings. St. John makes this rather clear: "The ten horns shall hate and devour the woman." And Daniel says: "I considered the horns, and behold, there came up among them another littler horn with eyes like the eyes of a man and a mouth speaking great things." That is the Antichrist.

Newman tries to determine how far these prophecies have been fulfilled, and what remains to be accomplished. The Roman empire did break up; it divided into a number of separate kingdoms—France, Germany, England, Italy, etc. Yet it is difficult to number the ten kingdoms accurately and exactly. Then, though Rome has been sacked often most fearfully, yet it has never suffered from ten parts of its own empire. Rather it has been brought down by barbarians who came from outside the empire. Moreover, Rome still exists today as a city, whereas it was to be "desolated, devoured and burned with fire." Finally, Rome has not as yet fulfilled another description of the city of Satan. She has not taken "the golden cup in her hand full of abominations," nor made "the inhabitants of the earth drunk with the wine of her fornication," expressions implying a successful world wide seduction. This she has not done to date.

The Roman Empire has not yet been divided into ten kingdoms, so the time for the Antichrist has not yet come. And all the Fathers say that the ten kingdoms are to come at the end of the world and last but a short time. Then the Antichrist will come upon them suddenly. Can one say today whether the Roman Empire is gone or still with us, however attenuated? In one sense it is gone, for it is divided into kingdoms. In another sense it is not, for the date cannot be assigned on which it came to an end, and much could be said for its continued existence, though this be a mutilated and decayed existence. The Roman Empire must some day revive for ten vigorous kingdoms must arise from her and be conquered by the Antichrist before the end comes.

The prophet describes the resurrection of Rome thus: "The beast," that is, the Roman Empire, "the monster that you saw, *was and is not*, and *shall* ascend out of the abyss *that was and is not and yet is*. Moreover, the ten kings and the empire will arise together, the kings appearing at the time of the monster's resurrection, not when it was languid and torpid. "The ten kings...have received no kingdom as yet, but receive power as kings one hour with the beast." If the Roman empire is still prostrate, the ten kings have not yet come, the destined destroyer of the woman, and the full judgements upon Rome, have not yet been realized."

However much she may have suffered throughout history, the full measure of God's judgement has not yet fallen upon Rome. It did fall upon Jerusalem, the holy city. That city and its people rejected God and Christ. God sent the Roman legions under the emperor, Titus, to destroy completely apostate Jerusalem and Israel. The divine vengeance fell upon the holy city, then turned against the Roman Empire which was disorganized, broken in pieces by insurrections, plagues, famines and earthquakes, while countless hosts of barbarians attacked it from all sides and even burned and pillaged Rome itself. Yet the Roman Empire and the city of Rome remained in existence. The Goth, the Hun, the Vandal plundered Rome, but did not annihilate her. Why has Rome been granted so far such special treatment in God's providence?

It was the consensus of serious thinkers in the early Church that the barbarian invasions were merely a preliminary punishment sent by God upon a wicked Roman Empire and city of Rome. In the end they predicted, God would completely destroy the city by the fury of the elements.

Gregory the Great wrote in his Dialogues: "Rome shall not be destroyed by the nations, but shall consume away internally, worn out by storms of lightning, whirlwinds and earthquakes." Yet Rome has not yet been wholly and irrevocably destroyed because God has always had a faithful people in that city. Babylon, Sodom and Gomorra were wholly rotten, hence wholly destroyed. But Rome received the Church as a guest. Christians dwelt there, suffered there, prayed there. They were the life and salt of the very city which persecuted them. St. Augustine used this same argument against his pagan brethren who blamed all the catastrophes that befell the empire and the city of Rome and the Christians. Augustine pointed to the cities which had sinned and had been visited with divine chastisements; he showed that they had perished altogether, whereas Rome was still preserved. Here, he said, was fulfillment of God's promise to Abraham; for the sake of the faithful Christians in it, Rome was chastised, but not utterly destroyed. Historical facts bear out the truth of his interpretation. Alaric, the fierce conqueror, arrived at the gates of defenseless Rome. Yet he exhorted his troops "to respect the churches of the Apostles St. Peter and St. Paul, as holy and inviolable sanctuaries." Fifty years later Attila the Hun advanced against the city. Pope St. Leo was successful in the arresting his plan to destroy the city. Then a few years later, came Genseric, the most savage of barbarian conquerors. Pope Leo again mitigated the fury of the barbarians. Though they pillaged the city, they kept their promise to the Pope to spare the unresisting multitude, and to protect the buildings from fire and the captives from torture. Here is displayed the wonderful rule of God's loving providence. The Church suffers daily with the world and in so doing sanctifies the world. Total divine vengeance is still suspended over the city of Rome because the Christian Church still lives, suffers, witnesses and dies a martyr's death there, interceding for the city, sanctifying and saving it.

Newman concludes that Rome may be spared until the end of time. Then, too, just as Babylon is a type of Rome and of the world of sin and vanity, so Rome in turn may be a type also, whether of some other city, or of the proud and entire deceiving world. The woman is said to be Babylon as well as Rome; so again she may be something more than Rome, a city of sin which is yet to come or is building towards being the capital of the Antichrist's empire. Perhaps the total ruin depicted by the prophets for the city of the Antichrist applies to the general wickedness of the whole world at the time of the Antichrist. Certainly tragic judgements came upon Rome when her empire was taken from her. Her persecutions of the Church have been in a large measure punished by God. Scripture's predictions about her have been fulfilled. Whether she is to be judged finally and destroyed utterly depends first on whether righteous men in the city will save her, and second, whether the prophecy of final, complete destruction relates in its fullness to Rome or to some other city of which Rome is a type. But if Rome is to be judged, this must be before the Antichrist destroys the ten kings. The ten kings are to destroy Rome and the Antichrist will last a short time in power. The prophecy, it seems, has not yet been fulfilled, whatever one decides about Rome. For the Roman empire has not yet been divided into ten kingdoms; it has not yet risen to devour the woman, whoever she stands for, nor has final judgment come crashing down upon the woman. At any rate and by any interpretation the city of the Antichrist will be a city plagued with sin; it will be a sacrilegious city, an idolatrous city, the mystical society of Satan upon the earth.

Chapter IV: *The Persecution of the Antichrist*

Persecutions are a characteristic mark of Christ's Church. They are not a necessary lot of the Church, but one of the appropriate badges, a sign by which one recognizes that she belongs to her crucified founder. Christ makes it clear that His Church is to have the same lot as He had. His life and hers in time begin and end in persecution. He ascended from her and left her in persecution; He will come back and find her in the worst persecution of all time. The prophets all speak of this most dreadful prosecution yet to come upon the Church. Christ Himself predicted it.

Then shall be great tribulation, such as was not since the

beginning of the world to this time, no, nor ever shall be; and unless these days had been shortened, no flesh would be saved; but for the sake of the elect, these days shall be shortened.

Some of the principal texts from Scripture that Newman uses to indicate the final worst persecution, that of the Antichrist, against the Church are as follows:

Another shall rise after them, and...he shall speak great words against the Most High, and shall wear out the saints of the Most High, and think to change times and laws; and they shall be given into his hand until a time, times and a dividing of time: that is three and one-half years.

They shall pollute the Sanctuary of strength, and shall take away the Daily Sacrifice, and they shall place the Abomination that makes desolate, and such as do wickedly against the Covenant shall be corrupted by flatteries; but the people that do know their God shall be strong and do exploits. And they that understand among the people shall instruct many; yet they shall fall by the sword and by flame, by captivity, by spoil many days.

Many shall be purified and made white and tried; but the wicked shall do wickedly...and from the time that the Daily Sacrifice shall be taken away, and the Abomination that makes desolate set up, there shall be a thousand two hundred and ninety days.

Then shall be great tribulation, such as was not since the beginning of the world.

The beast that ascends out of the bottomless pit shall make war against them and shall overcome and kill them....And they that dwell upon the earth shall rejoice over them and make merry and shall send gifts one to another because these two prophets tormented them that dwell on the earth.

And the woman fled into the wilderness where she has a place prepared of God, that they should feed her there a thousand two hundred and threescore days.

And there was given unto him a mouth speaking great things and blasphemies; and power was given unto him to continue forty and two months. And he opened his mouth in blasphemy against God, to blaspheme His name and His tabernacle and them that dwell in heaven. And it was given unto him to make war with the saints and to overcome them...and all that dwell upon the earth shall worship him, whose names are not written in the book of life of the Lamb slain from the foundation of the world.

I saw an Angel come down from heaven, having the key of the bottomless pit and a great chain in his hand; and he laid hold on the dragon, that old serpent, which is the devil and Satan, and bound him a thousand years...and after that he must be loosed a little season...and shall go out to deceive the nations which are in the four quarters of the earth, Gog and Magog, to gather them together to battle: the number of whom is as the sand of the sea. And they went up on the breadth of the earth and compassed the camp of the saints about and the beloved city.

The early Christians interpreted these passages as terrifying persecution which the Antichrist would inflict on the Church in the last days. All previous persecutions were considered pallid preludes to the final tribulations. For in all previous persecutions the Church had also been somewhat sheltered in various places. In the final, universal persecution she will have no place to hide. Moreover, never before was a persecution attended with the cessation of all religious worship. But in the final trials, "they shall take away the Daily Sacrifice," words which the early Fathers interpreted to mean that the Antichrist will suppress for three and a half years all public religious worship. Instead the Antichrist will have himself set up, in the symbol of the statue struck in his image and likeness and miraculously made to move and speak by the power of Satan, in the restored Temple of Jerusalem, there to receive the adoration and other honors from his idolatrous followers. But the last and worst persecution will be advanced with a marvelous eruption of "lying wonders," miracles more stupendous than those the magicians of Egypt effected with Satan's power against Moses. Whether these miracles are real or pretended, or the result of the Antichrist's virtuosity in manipulating the forces of science makes little difference. For they will produce in the masses the same effect as if they were genuine miracles. They will overpower the imaginations and wills of millions who will decide to abandon the true God and follow the Antichrist. "There will be signs and wonders," says Our Lord, "inasmuch that, if it were possible, they shall deceive the very elect." And St. Paul speaks of the Antichrist as one:

whose coming is after the working of Satan, with all power and signs and lying wonders, and with all deception of unrighteousness in them that perish, because they received not the love of truth, that they might be saved. And for this cause God shall send them strong delusion that they should believe a lie.

And St. John:

He does great wonders so that he makes fire come down from heaven on the earth in the sight of men and deceives them that dwell on the earth by the means of those miracles which he had power to do in the sight of the beast. Newman thus lists four aspects of the final persecution mounted by the Antichrist. It will be fiercer, more horrible, more aweful than all earlier persecutions taken singularly or collectively. It will effect the cessation of the ordinances of grace, especially of the Daily Sacrifice. It will set up the open, legal establishment of infidelity coupled with a blasphemous, habitual way of life even within the holiest recesses of the

Church. It will be supported and advanced with a marvelous power of working miracles. Then Newman goes on to comment on the first aspect alone, that is, the sharpness, cruelty and universality of the trials.

A brief survey of the history of the Church will convince any reader that cruelties more shocking than those suffered by the early Christians are almost unimaginable before the event. Even St. Paul's recording of the persecutions before his time do but weakly describe the trials the Church suffered in his day and afterwards. Jewish saints were tortured, mocked, scourged, imprisoned, stoned, sawn asunder, tempted, slain with the sword, driven out to wander in sheepskins and goatskins, left destitute, afflicted, abandoned. These were the persecutions visited on the faithful prophets under the Law. As they anticipated the Gospel in doctrine, so did they anticipate the Gospel in sufferings. But the persecutions against the Gospel were much sharper, even as the Gospel doctrine was much clearer.

Newman than relates the bloodcurdling martyrdom of Sts. Sanctus, Maturus, Attalus and Blandina. They were tortured by turns in every possible way from morning till evening, their bodies being burnt, mangled and pierced in every part. But their constancy in the faith exhausted their persecutors. Then red-hot plates were fastened to the tenderest parts of the body. But they still survived their sufferings and grew more radiant in the faith. Some days later they were taken to the games and went through every torture again, as if they had suffered nothing before. Scourged, forced into red-hot iron chairs, dragged around by the beasts, they finally came to their victorious end. Blandina, however, was hung on a cross, placed so as to be devoured by the beasts turned loose on her. Then scourged, she was placed in a basket, thrown to a bull and died under the tossing of the furious animal. Then Newman briefly relates the unspeakable tortures the arian Vandals inflicted on four hundred bishops of Africa, and ten years later, two hundred and twenty more; and later still on some four thousand Christians faithful to the orthodox creed. Hard labor in unhealthy places, exile, long marches across burning sands, torture, laceration with scourges, burnings with hot irons, the cutting off of limbs, these were but some of the tortures that preceded their violent deaths. Yet even these supreme tortures did not prevent the early Fathers from predicting far worse cruelties for the Church in the days of the Antichrist.

It is certain that the final persecution has not yet come and that we must therefore prepare for its arrival. All ages in the Church have been convinced that Scripture has foretold this coming catastrophe. Every generation of Christians has been on the watch, looking out more anxiously as time advances. Signs do occur in history from time to time, not to fix the day, but to remind us that the Antichrist and the final struggle between the Church and her enemies is daily approaching. Other signs tell us that the universe and the planets are growing old; our earth keeps crumbling away under the forces of nature and the abuse of man. The night is far spent; the day is at hand. Shadows begin to move; the old forms of the Roman empire, with us from the time of Christ, heave, tremble, and nod toward a fall. When they go, the Antichrist will be released, announced and acclaimed. But he will disappear in a short, fearful season. And then Christ will come in power and glory.

One might use the analogy of a man slowly dying on his bed for the present condition of the Roman empire. It exists and yet does not exist. It has relapses, recoveries, days of coma and days of consciousness. It is not dead yet on its deathbed; it lingers, rallies, fails. It is a matter of time; the illness is terminal, but the exact day of demise is uncertain. It will die, no doubt, with some violence and convulsions. The Antichrist is the head of this empire, but the empire must finally die to make way for his ascendency to full power. Thus death is hastening forward, surely, irrevocably, whether it takes a few years more or less. It may come after our time or that of our children, for we are all creatures of a day and a generation is like the striking of a clock. But the empire, the world, human society are tending to dissolution; their days are fast running out, ever decreasing in numbers.

Another anxious sign that Newman took as an indication of the approaching power of the Antichrist was that in his day the power of Islam was visibly declining. Lastly, he mentions another remarkable token of the approaching end. Referring to the Apocalypse, he recalls that it is predicted that in the last persecution Satan will be loosed from his prison, will deceive the nations, God and Magog, and unite them all in a war against the Church. Newman observes, moreover, that the northern nations will be stirred up against the Church. This has happened twice already. First the Goths and Vandals attacked the Church and became Arian heretics. Second, the Turks attacked the Church after they were deceived into the false religion of Islam. Were these nations the shadows of the Gog and Magog to come in the future? Newman thought that perhaps they were. At any rate, he saw in his day the nations of the North gathering strength as never before; and these nations were bitter enemies of the Church. This he took as a sign of the advance of the Antichrist; it was perhaps only a preparation, a warning, a call to sober thought on things to come; perhaps it was only a cloud in the sky warning about the advancing storm.

Newman concludes his comments on the last persecution, the persecution of the Antichrist thus: It may not be a persecution of blood and death, but of craft and subtlety— not of miracles but of natural wonders and marvels of human skill, human acquirements in the hands of the devil. Satan may adopt the more alarming weapons of deceit- he may seduce us in little things, move the Church, not all at once, but little by little from her true position. He has had much success in this tactic in the last centuries. He has moved every part of the Church away from the truth of Christ, from the old faith upon which it was built. It is Satan's policy to split us and divide us, to dislodge us gradually from the rock of strength. When he has divided the whole of Christendom, the final persecution may come. When we were full of schism and heresy, what better time for the appearance of the Antichrist? When Christians have flung themselves into the arms of the world, Christ's enemy, when they depend for their protection on the world and have surrendered their independence, honor and strength to its approval, then will the Antichrist burst upon them in fury, then will the idolatrous nations open the flood gates of wickedness and overrun the Church and the world with the hatred and cruelty that is let loose from the abyss of hell. Then will Satan and the Antichrist have their hour, their last hour of darkness upon the earth. For they and their wicked followers will suddenly disappear into the never-ending darkness of eternal perdition.

Fr. Vincent P. Miceli, S.J.

I

The Times of Antichrist

The Thessalonian Christians had supposed that the coming of Christ was near at hand. St. Paul writes to warn them against such an expectation. Not that he discountenances their looking out for our Lord's coming,—the contrary; but he tells them that a certain event must come before it, and till that was arrived, the end would not be. "Let no man deceive you by any means," he says; "for that Day shall not come, except there come a falling away first,"—and he proceeds "and" except first "that man of sin be revealed, the son of perdition."

As long as the world lasts, this passage of Scripture will be full of reverent interest to Christians. It is their duty ever to be watching for the advent of their Lord, to search for the signs of it in all that happens around them; and above all to keep in mind this great and awful sign of which St. Paul speaks to the Thessalonians. As our Lord's first coming had its forerunner, so will the second have its own. The first was "One more than a prophet," the Holy Baptist: the second will be more than an enemy of Christ; it will be the very image of Satan, the fearful and hateful Antichrist. Of

1

him, as described in prophecy, I propose to speak; and, in doing so, I shall follow the exclusive guidance of the ancient Fathers of the Church.

I follow the ancient Fathers, not as thinking that on such a subject they have the weight they possess in the instance of doctrines or ordinances. When they speak of doctrines, they speak of them as being universally held. They are witnesses to the fact of those doctrines being received, not here or there, but everywhere. We receive those doctrines which they thus teach, not merely because they teach them, but because they bear witness that all Christians everywhere then held them. We take them as honest informants, but not as a sufficient authority in themselves, though they are an authority too. If they were to state these very same doctrines, but say, "These are our opinions: we deduced them from Scripture, and they are true," we might well doubt about receiving them at their hands. We might fairly say, that we had as much right to deduce from Scripture as they had; that deductions of Scripture were mere opinions; that if our deductions agreed with theirs, that would be a happy coincidence, and increase our confidence in them; but if they did not, it could not be helped—we must follow our own light. Doubtless no man has any right to impose his own deductions upon another, in matters of faith. There is an obvious obligation, indeed, upon the ignorant to submit to those who are better informed; and there is a fitness in the young submitting implicitly for a time to the teaching of their elders; but beyond this, one man's opinion is not better than the another's. But this is not the state of the case as regards the primitive Fathers. They do not speak of their *own private* opinion; they do not say, "This is true *because* we see it in Scripture—about which there might be differences in judgments—but, "this is true, because in matter of fact it is held, and has ever been held, by all the Churches, down to our times, without interruption, ever since the Apostles:" where the question is merely one of testimony, whether they had the means of knowing that it had been and was so held; for if it was the belief of so many and independent Churches at once, and that as if from the Apostles, doubtless it cannot but be true and Apostolic.

This, I say is the mode in which the Fathers speak as regards *doctrine*; but it is otherwise when they interpret prophecy. In this matter there seems to have been no catholic, no formal and distinct, or at least no authoritative traditions; so that when they interpret Scripture, they are for the most part giving, and profess to be giving, either their own private opinions, or vague, floating, and merely general anticipations. This is what might have been expected; for it is not ordinarily the course of Divine Providence to interpret prophecy before the event. What the Apostles disclosed concerning the future, was for the most part disclosed by them in private, to individuals—not committed to writing, not intended for the edifying of the body of Christ,—and was soon lost. Thus, in a few verses after the text, St. Paul says, "Remember ye not, that when I was yet with you, I told you these things?" and he writes by hints and allusions, not speaking out. And it shows how little care was taken to discriminate and authenticate his prophetical intimations, that the Thessalonians had adopted an opinion, that he had said—what in fact he had not said—that the day of Christ was immediately at hand.

Yet, though the Fathers do not convey to us the interpretation of prophecy with the same certainty as they convey doctrine, yet, in proportion to their agreement, their personal weight, and the prevalence, or again the authoritative character of the opinions they are stating, they are to be read with deference; for, to say the least, they are as likely to be right as commentators now; in some respects more so, because the interpretation of prophecy has become in these times a matter of controversy and party. And passion and prejudice have so interfered with soundness of judgment, that it is difficult to say who is to be trusted in it, or whether a private Christian may not be as good an expositor as those by whom the office has been assumed.

1.

Now to turn to the passage in question, which I shall examine by arguments drawn from Scripture, without being

4

solicitous to agree, or to say why I am at issue with modern commentators: "That day shall not come, except there come a falling away first." Here the sign of the second Advent is said to be a certain frightful apostasy, and the manifestation of the man of sin, the son of perdition,—that is, as he is commonly called, Antichrist. Our Savior seems to add, that the sign will immediately precede Him, or that His coming will follow close upon it; for after speaking of "false prophets" and "false Christs," "showing signs and wonders," "iniquity abounding," and "love waxing cold," and the like, He adds, "When ye shall see all these things, know that it is near, even at the doors." Again He says, "When ye shall see the Abomination of Desolation… stand in the holy place… then let them that be in Judea flee into the mountains" (Matt. xxiv. 16, 33). Indeed, St. Paul implies this also, when he says that Antichrist shall be destroyed by the brightness of Christ's coming.

First then, I say, if Antichrist is to come *immediately* before Christ, and to be the sign of His coming, it is manifest that Antichrist is not come yet, but is still to be expected; for, else Christ would have come before now.

Further, it appears that the time of Antichrist's tyranny will be three years and a half, or, as Scripture expresses it, "a time, and times, and a dividing of time," or "forty-two months,"—which is an additional reason for believing he is not come; for, if so, he must have come quite lately, his time

5

being altogether so short; that is, within the last three years, and this we cannot say he has.

Besides, there are two other circumstances of his appearance, which have not been fulfilled. First, a time of unexampled trouble. "Then shall be great tribulation, such as was not from the beginning of the world to this time, no, nor ever shall be; and except those days should be shortened, there should no flesh be saved" (*Ib.* 21,22). This has not yet been. Next, the preaching of the Gospel throughout the world— "And this Gospel of the kingdom shall be preached in all the world for a witness unto all nations; and then shall the end come" (*Ib.* 14).

2.

Now it may be objected to this conclusion, that St. Paul says, in the passage before us, that "the mystery of iniquity doth already work," that is, even in *his* day, as if Antichrist had in fact come even then. But he would seem to mean merely this, that in his day there were shadows and forebodings, earnests, and operative elements, of that which was one day to come in its fullness. Just as the types of Christ went before Christ, so the shadows of Antichrist precede him. In truth, every event in this world is a type of those that follow, history proceeding forward as a circle ever enlarging. The days of the Apostles typified the last days: there were false Christs, and risings, and troubles, and persecutions and the judicial destruction of the Jewish Church. In like manner every age presents its own picture of those future events, which, and which alone, are the real fulfillment of the prophecy which stands at the head of all of them. Hence St. John says, "Little children, it is the last time; and as ye have heard that the Antichrist shall come, *even now* are there many Antichrists; whereby we know that it is the last time" (1 John ii. 18). Antichrist was come, and was not come; it was, and it was not the last time. In the sense in which the Apostles' day might be called the "last time," and the end of the world, it was also the time of Antichrist.

A second objection may be made as follows: St. Paul says, "Now ye know what withholdeth, that he (Antichrist) might be revealed in his time." Here a something is mentioned as keeping back the manifestation of the enemy of truth. He proceeds: "He that now withholdeth, will withhold, until he be taken out the way." Now this restraining power was in early times considered to be the Roman Empire, but the Roman Empire (it is argued) has long been taken out of the way; it follows that Antichrist has long since come. In answer to this objection, I would grant that he "that withholdeth," or "hindereth," means the power of Rome, for all the ancient writers so speak of it. I grant that as Rome, according to the prophet Daniel's vision, succeeded Greece, so Antichrist succeeds Rome, and the Second Coming succeeds Antichrist (Chrysostom *in loco*). But it does not

7

hence follow that Antichrist is come: for it is not clear that the Roman empire is gone. Far from it: the Roman Empire in the view of prophecy, remains even to this day. Rome had a very different fate from the other three monsters mentioned by the Prophet, as will be seen by his description of it. "Behold a fourth beast, dreadful and terrible, and strong exceedingly; and it had great iron teeth: it devoured and brake in pieces, and stamped the residue with the feet of it: and it *was diverse from all the beasts that* were before it, and it *had ten horns*" (Dan. vii. 7). These ten horns, an Angel informed him, "are ten kings that shall arise out of this kingdom" of Rome. As, then, the ten horns belonged to the fourth beast, and were not separate from it, so the kingdoms into which the Roman Empire was to be divided, are but the continuation and termination of that Empire itself,—which lasts on, and in some sense lives in the view of prophecy, however we decide the historical question. Consequently, we have not *yet* seen the end of the Roman Empire. "That which withholdeth" still exists, up to the manifestation of its ten horns; and till it is removed, Antichrist will not come. And from the midst of those horns he will arise, as the same Prophet informs us: "I considered the horns, and behold, there came up among them another little horn; … and behold in this horn were eyes like the eyes of a man, and a mouth speaking great things."

Up to the time, then, when Antichrist shall actually appear, there has been and will be a continual effort to manifest him to the world on the part of the powers of evil. The history of the Church is the history of that long birth. "The mystery of iniquity doth *already* work," says St. Paul. "*Even now* there are many Antichrists" (1 John ii. 18), says St. John— "every spirit that confesseth not that Jesus Christ is come in the flesh, is not of God; and *this* is that spirit of the Antichrist, whereof ye have heard that it should come, *and even now already is it in the world*" (*Ib.* iv. 3). It has been at work ever since, from that time of the Apostles, though kept under by him that "withholdeth." At this very time there is a fierce struggle, the spirit of Antichrist attempting to rise, and the political power in those countries which are prophetically Roman, firm and vigorous in repressing it. And in fact, we actually have before our eyes, as our fathers also in the generation before us, a fierce and lawless principle everywhere at work—a spirit of rebellion against God and man, which the powers of government in each country can barely keep under with their greatest efforts. Whether this which we witness *be* that spirit of Antichrist, which is one day at length to be let loose, this ambitious spirit, the parent of all heresy, schism, sedition, revolution, and war— whether this be so or not, at least we know from prophecy that the present framework of society and government, as far as it is the representative of Roman powers, is that which withholdeth, and Antichrist is that which will rise when this restraint fails.

3.

It has been more or less implied in the foregoing remarks, that Antichrist is one man, an individual, not a power or a kingdom. Such surely is the impression left on the mind by the Scripture notices concerning him, after taking fully into account the figurative character of prophetical language; and such was the universal belief of the early Church. Consider these passages together, which describe him, and see whether we must not so conclude. First, the passage in St. Paul's Epistle: "That day shall not come, except there come a falling away first, and that man of sin be revealed, the son of perdition, who is the adversary and rival of all that is called God or worshipped; so that he sitteth as God in the temple of God, proclaiming himself to be God…. Then shall that Wicked One be revealed, whom the Lord shall consume with the spirit of His mouth, and shall destroy with the brightness of His coming… whose coming is after the working of Satan, with all power and signs and lying wonders."

Next, in the prophet Daniel: "Another shall rise after them, and he shall be diverse from the first, and he shall subdue three kings. And he shall speak great words against the Most High, and shall wear out the saints of the Most High, and think to change times and laws: and they shall be given into his hand until a time and times, and the dividing of the time. But the judgment shall sit, and they shall take away his dominion, to consume and to destroy it unto the end." Again: "And the king shall do according to his will; and he shall exalt and magnify himself above every god, and shall speak marvelous things against the God of gods and shall prosper till the indignation be accomplished…. Neither shall he regard the God of his fathers, nor the Desire of women, nor regard any god; for he shall magnify himself above all. But in his estate shall he honor the God of forces, and a God whom his fathers knew not shall he honor with gold and silver, and with precious stones and pleasant things" (Dan. vii. xi). Let it be observed, that Daniel elsewhere describes other kings, and that the event has shown them certainly to be individuals,—for instance, Xerxes, Darius, and Alexander.

And in like manner St. John: "There was given unto him a mouth speaking great things, and blasphemies; and power was given unto him to continue forty and two months. And he opened his mouth in blasphemy against God, to blaspheme s Name, and His tabernacle, and them that dwell in heaven. And it was given unto him to make war with the saints, and to overcome them; and power was given him over all kindreds and tongues and nations. And all that dwell upon the earth shall worship him, whose names are not written in the book of life of the Lamb slain from the foundation of the world" (Rev. xiii).

Further, that by Antichrist is meant some one person, is made probable by the anticipations, which have already occurred in history, of the fulfillment of the prophecy. Individual men have arisen actually answering in a great measure to the above descriptions; and this circumstance creates a probability, that the absolute and entire fulfillment which is to come will be in an individual also. The most remarkable of these shadows of the destined scourge appeared before the time of the Apostles, between them and the age of Daniel, viz. the heathen king Antiochus, of whom we read in the book of Maccabees. This instance is the more to the purpose, because he is actually described, (as we suppose) by Daniel, in another part of his prophecy, in terms which seem also to belong to Antichrist, and as belonging, imply that Antiochus was what he seems to be, a type of that more fearful future enemy of the Church. This Antiochus was the savage persecutor of the Jews, in their latter times, as Antichrist will be of the Christians. A few passages from the Maccabees will show you what he was. St. Paul in the text speaks of an Apostasy, and of Antichrist as following upon it; and thus is the future of the Christian Church typified in the past Jewish history. "In those days went there out of Israel wicked men, who persuaded many, saying, Let us go and make a covenant with the heathen that are round about us: for since we departed from them, we have had much sorrow. So this device pleased them well. Then certain of the people were so forward herein, that they went to the king, who gave them license to do after the ordinances of the heathen; whereupon they built a place of exercise at Jerusalem, according to the custom of the heathen; and made themselves uncircumcised, and forsook the holy covenant, and joined themselves to the heathen, and were sold to do mischief." Here was the Falling away. After this introduction the Enemy of truth appears. "After that Antiochus had smitten Egypt, he returned again,… and went up against Israel and Jerusalem with a great multitude, and entered proudly into the sanctuary, and took away the golden altar, and the candlestick of light and all the vessels thereof, and the table of the shewbread, and the pouring vessels, and the vials, and the censers of gold, and the veil, and the crowns, and the golden ornaments that were before the temple, all which he pulled off. And when he had taken all away, he went into his own land, having made a great massacre, and spoken very proudly." After this, he set fire to Jerusalem, "and pulled down the houses and walls thereof on every side…. Then built they the city of David, with a great and strong wall,… and they put therein a sinful nation, wicked men, and fortified themselves therein." Next, "King Antiochus wrote to his whole kingdom, that all should be one people, and every one should leave his laws: so all the heathen agreed according to the commandment of the king. Yea, many also of the Israelites consented to his religion, and sacrificed unto idols, and profaned the sabbath." After this he forced these impieties upon the chosen people. All were to be put to death who would not "profane the Sabbath and festival days, and pollute the sanctuary and holy people: and set up altars, and groves, and chapels of idols, and sacrifice swine's flesh and unclean beasts," and "leave their children uncircumcised." At length he set up an idol, or in the words of the history, "the Abomination of Desolation upon the altar, and builded idol altars throughout the cities of Juda on every side…. And when they had rent in pieces the books of the law which they found, they burnt them with fire." It is added, "Howbeit many in Israel were fully resolved and confirmed in themselves not to eat any unclean thing, wherefore they choose rather to die… and there was very great wrath upon Israel" (1 Mac. i). Here we have presented to us some of the lineaments of Antichrist, who will be such, and worse than such, as Antiochus.

The history of the apostate emperor Julian, who lived between 300 and 400 years after Christ, furnishes another approximation to the predicted Antichrist, and an additional reason for thinking he will be one person, not a kingdom, power, or the like.

So again does the false prophet Mahomet, who propagated his imposture about 600 years after Christ came.

Lastly, that Antichrist is one individual man, not a power,— not a mere ethical spirit, or a political system, not a dynasty, or succession of rulers,—was the universal tradition of the early Church. "We must say," writes St. Jerome upon Daniel, "what has been handed down to us by all ecclesiastical

14

writers, that, in the end of the world, when the Roman Empire is to be destroyed, there will be ten kinds, to divide the Roman territory between them, and that an eleventh will rise up, a small kind, who will subdue three of the ten, and thereupon receive the submission of the other seven. It is said that 'the Horn had eyes, as the eyes of a man,' lest we should, as some have thought, suppose him to be the evil spirit, or a demon, whereas he is one man, in whom Satan shall dwell bodily. 'And a mouth speaking great things;' for he is the man of sin, the son of perdition, so that he dares to 'sit in the Temple of God, making himself as if God.' 'The beast has been slain, and his carcase has perished;' since Antichrist blasphemes in that united Roman Empire, all its kingdoms are at one and the same time to be abolished, and there shall be no earthly kingdom, but the society of the saints, and the coming of the triumphant Son of God." And Theodoret: "Having spoken of Antiochus Epiphanes, the prophet passes from the figure to the Antitype; for the Antitype of Antiochus is Antichrist, and the figure of Antichrist is Antiochus. As Antiochus compelled the Jews to act impiously, so the Man of Sin, the son of perdition, will make every effort for the seduction of the pious, by false miracles, and by force, and by persecution. As the Lord says, 'Then will be great tribulation, such as never was from the beginning of the world till this time, nor ever shall be" (Jerom. in Dat. vii; Theodo. in Dan. xi).

What I have said upon this subject may be summed up as follows:—that the coming of Christ will be immediately preceded by a very awful and unparalleled outbreak of evil, called by St. Paul an Apostasy, a falling away, in the midst of which a certain terrible Man of sin and Child of perdition, the special and singular enemy of Christ, or Antichrist, will appear; that this will be when revolutions prevail, and the present framework of society breaks to pieces; that at present the spirit which he will embody and represent is kept under by "the powers that be," but that on their dissolution, he will rise out of the bosom of them, and knit them together again in his own evil way, under his own rule, to the exclusion of the Church.

4.

It would be out of place to say more than this at present. I will but insist on one particular circumstance contained in the St. Paul's announcement which I have already in part commented on.

It is said there will "come a falling away, and the man of sin will be revealed." In other words, the Man of Sin is born of an Apostasy, or at least comes into power through an apostasy, or is preceded by an apostasy, or would not be except for an apostasy. So says the inspired text: now observe, how remarkably the course of Providence, as seen in history, has commented on this prediction.

16

First, we have a comment in the instance of Antiochus previous to the actual events contemplated in the prophecy. The Israelites, or at least great numbers of them, put off their own sacred religion, *and then* the enemy was allowed to come in.

Next the apostate emperor Julian, who attempted to overthrow the Church by craft, and introduce paganism back again: it is observable that he was preceded, nay, he was nurtured, by heresy; by that first great heresy which disturbed the peace and purity of the Church. About forty years before he became emperor, arose the pestilent Arian heresy which denied that Christ was God. It ate its way among the rulers of the Church like a canker, and what with the treachery of some and the mistakes of others, at one time it was all but dominant throughout Christendom. The few holy and faithful men, who witnessed for the Truth, cried out, with awe and terror at the apostasy, that Antichrist was coming. They called it the "forerunner of Antichrist." ("Now is the Apostasy; for men have fallen away from the right faith. This then is the Apostasy, and the enemy must be looked out for." —Cyril. *Catech.*, 15. n. 9.) And true, his Shadow came. Julian was educated in the bosom of Arianism by some of its principle upholders. His tutor was the Eusebius from whom its partisans took their name; and in due time he fell away to paganism, became a hater and persecuted of the Church, and was cut off before he had reigned out the brief period which will be the real Antichrist's duration.

And thirdly, another heresy arose, a heresy in its consequences far more lasting and far spreading; it was of twofold character; with two heads, as I may call them, Nestorianism and Eutychianism, apparently opposed to each other, yet acting towards a common end: both in one way or other denied the truth of Christ's gracious incarnation, and tended to destroy the faith of Christians not less certainly, though more insidiously, than the heresy of Arius. It spread through the East and through Egypt, corrupting and poisoning those Churches which had once, alas! been the most flourishing, the early abodes and the strongholds of revealed truth. Out of this heresy, or at least by means of it, the imposter Mahomet sprang, and formed his creed. Here is another especial shadow of Antichrist.

These instances give us warning:—Is the enemy of Christ, and His Church, to arise out of a certain special falling away from God? And is there no reason to fear that some such Apostasy is gradually preparing, gathering, hastening on in this very day? For is there not at this very time a special effort made almost all over the world, that is, every here and there, more or less, in sight or out of sight, in this or that place, but mostly visibly or formidably in its most civilized and powerful parts, an effort to do without Religion? Is there not an opinion avowed and growing, that nation has nothing to do with Religion; that it is merely a matter for each man's own conscience,—which is all one with saying that we may let the Truth fail from the earth without trying to continue it in and on after our time. Is there not a vigorous and united movement in all countries to cast down the Church of Christ from power and place? Is there not a feverish and ever busy endeavor to get rid of the necessity of Religion in public transactions? for example, an attempt to get rid of oaths, under a pretence that they are too sacred for affairs of common life, instead of providing that they be taken more reverently and more suitably? An attempt to educate without Religion?—that is, by putting all forms of Religion together, which comes to the same thing;—an attempt to enforce temperance, and the virtues which flow from it, without Religion, by means of Societies which are built on mere principles of utility? An attempt to make *expedience*, and not *truth* the end and the rule of measures of State and the enactments of Law? an attempt to make numbers, and not the Truth, the ground of maintaining, or not maintaining, this or that creed, as if we had any reason whatever in Scripture for thinking that the many will be in the right, and the few in the wrong? An attempt to deprive the Bible of its one meaning to the exclusion of other, to make people think that it may have an hundred meanings all equally good, or, in other words, that it has no meaning at all, is a dead letter, and may be put aside? an attempt to supersede Religion altogether, as far as it is external or objective, as far as it is displayed in ordinances, or can be expressed by written words,—to confine it to our inward feelings, and thus, considering how variable, how evanescent our feelings are, and attempt in fact, to destroy Religion?

Surely, there is at this day a confederacy of evil, marshalling its hosts from all parts of the world, organizing itself, taking its measures, enclosing the Church of Christ as in a net, and preparing the way for a general Apostasy from it. Whether this very Apostasy is to give birth to Antichrist, or whether he is still to be delayed, as he has already been delayed so long, we cannot know; but at any rate this Apostasy, and all its tokens and instruments, are of the Evil One and savor of death. Far be it from any of us to be of those simple ones, who are taken in that snare which is circling around us! Far be it from us to be seduced with the fair promises in which Satan is sure to hide his poison! Do you think he is so unskillful in his craft, as to ask you openly and plainly to join him in his warfare against the Truth? No; he offers you baits to tempt you. He promises you civil liberty; he promises you equality; he promises you trade and wealth; he promises you a remission of taxes; he promises you reform. This is the way in which he conceals from you the kind of work to which he is putting you; he tempts you to rail against your rulers and superiors; he does so himself, and induces you to imitate him; or he promises you illumination,—he offers you knowledge, science, philosophy, enlargement of mind. He scoffs at times gone by; he scoffs at every institution which reveres them.

He prompts you what to say, and then listens to you, and praises you and encourages you. He bids you mount aloft. He shows you how to become as gods. Then he laughs and jokes with you, and gets intimate with you; he takes your hand, and gets his fingers between yours, and grasps them, and then you are his.

Shall we Christians allow ourselves to have lot or part in this matter? Shall we, even with our little finger help on the Mystery of iniquity which is travailing for birth, and convulsing the earth with its pangs? "O my soul, come not thou into their secret; unto their assembly, mine honor, be not thou united." "What fellowship hath righteousness with unrighteousness? and what communion hath light with darkness? Wherefore, come out from among them, and be ye separate,"… lest you be workers together with God's enemies, and be opening the way for the Man of sin, the son of perdition.

II

The Religion of Antichrist

St. John tells us that "every spirit that confesseth not that Jesus Christ is come in the flesh, is that spirit of Antichrist, which even now already is in the world." It was the characteristic of the Antichrist, that he should openly deny our Lord Jesus Christ to be the Son of God come in the flesh from heaven. So exactly and fully was this description to answer to him, that to deny Christ might be suitably called the spirit of Antichrist, to be like Antichrist, to be Antichrists. The same thing is stated in a former chapter. "Who is the Liar but he that denieth that Jesus is the Christ? He is the Antichrist, that denieth the Father and the Son. Whosoever denieth the Son, the same hath not the Father" (1 John ii. 22, 23); from which words, moreover, it would appear that Antichrist will be led on from rejecting the Son of God, to the rejection of God altogether, either by implication or practically.

I shall now make some further observations on the characteristic marks of the predicted enemy of the Church; and, as in those I made last week, I shall confine myself to the interpretations of Scripture given by the early Fathers.

My reason for doing so is simply this,—that on so difficult a subject as unfulfilled prophecy, I really can have no opinion of my own, nor indeed is it desirable I should have, or at least that I should put it forward in any formal way. The opinion of any one person, even if he were the most fit to form one, could hardly be of any authority, or be worth putting forward by itself; whereas the judgment and views of the early Church claim and attract our especial regard, because for what we know they may be in part derived from traditions of the Apostles, and because they are put forward far more consistently and unanimously than those of any other set of teachers. Thus they have at least greater claims on our attention than those of other writers, be their claims little or great; if they are little, those of others are still less. The only really strong claim which can be made on our belief, is the clear fulfillment of the prophecy. Did we see all the marks of the prophecy satisfactorily answered in the past history of the Church, then we might dispense with authority in the parties setting the proof before us. This condition, however, can hardly be satisfied, because the date of Antichrist comes close upon the coming of Christ in judgment, and therefore the event will not have happened under such circumstances as to allow of being appealed to. Nor indeed is any history producible in which are fulfilled all the marks of Antichrist clearly, though some are fulfilled here and there. Nothing then is left us, (if we are to take up any opinion at all,—if we are to profit, as Scripture surely intends, by its warnings concerning the evil which is to come,) but to go by the judgment of the Fathers, whether that be of special authority in this matter or not. To them therefore I have had recourse already, and now shall have recourse again. To continue, then, the subject with the early Fathers as my guides.

1.

It seems clear the St. Paul and St. John speak of the same enemy of the Church, from the similarity of their descriptions. They both say, that the spirit itself was already at work in their day. "That spirit of the Antichrist," says St. John in the text, "is *now already* in the world." "The mystery of iniquity doth *already* work," says St. Paul. And they both describe the enemy as characterized by the same especial sin, open infidelity. St. John says, that "he is the Antichrist that *denieth the Father and the Son;*" while St. Paul speaks of him in like manner as "*the adversary and rival of all that is called God, or worshipped;*" that "he sitteth as God in the Temple of God, setting forth himself that he is God." In both these passages, the same blasphemous denial of God and religion is described; but St. Paul adds, in addition, that he will oppose all existing religion, true or false, "*all* that is called God, or worshipped."

Two other passages of Scripture may be adduced, predicting the same reckless impiety; one from the eleventh chapter of Daniel: "The king shall do according to his will; and he shall exalt himself and magnify himself *above every god*, and shall speak marvelous things *against the God of gods*, and shall prosper till the indignation be accomplished.... Neither shall he regard the *God of his fathers*, nor the Desire of women, nor *regard any god* —for he shall magnify himself *above all*."

The other passage is faintly marked with any prophetic allusion in itself, except that all our Savior's sayings have a deep meaning, and the Fathers take this in particular to have such. "I am come in My Father's Name, and ye receive Me not; if *another shall come in his own name*, him ye will receive" (1 John v. 43). This they consider to be a prophetic allusion to Antichrist, whom the Jews were to mistake for the Christ. He is to come "in *His own* name." Not from God, as even the Son of God came, who if any might have come in the power of His essential divinity, not in God's Name, not with any pretence of a mission from Him, but in his own name, by a blasphemous assumption of divine power, thus will Antichrist come.

To the above passages may be added those which speak generally of the impieties of the last age of the world, impieties which we may believe will usher in and be completed in Antichrist: —

"Many shall run to and fro, and knowledge shall be

increased…. Many shall be purified, and made white, and tried: but the wicked shall do wickedly; and none of the wicked shall understand, but the wise shall understand" (Daniel xii. 4, 10). "In the last days perilous times shall come, for men shall be lovers of their own selves, covetous, boasters, proud, blasphemers, disobedient to parents, unthankful, unholy, without natural affection, trucebreakers, false accusers, incontinent, fierce, despisers of those that are good, traitors, heady, high-minded, lovers of pleasures more than lovers of God, having a form of godliness but denying the power thereof" (2 Tim. iii. 2-5): "scoffers walking after their own lusts, and saying, Where is the promise of His coming?" (2 Pet. iii. 3, 4) "despising government, presumptuous….self-willed, not afraid to speak evil of dignities…promising men liberty, while themselves the servants of corruption" (2 Pet. ii. 10, 19): and the like.

2.

I just now made mention of the Jews: it may be well then to state what was held in the early Church concerning Antichrist's connection with them.

Our Lord foretold that many should come in His name, saying "I am Christ." It was the judicial punishment of the Jews, as of all unbelievers in one way or another, that having rejected the true Christ, they should take up with a false one; and Antichrist will be the complete and perfect seducer, towards whom all previous ones are approximations, according to the text just quoted, "If another shall come in his own name, him ye will receive." To the same purport are St. Paul's words after describing Antichrist; "whose coming," he says, "is...with all deceivableness of unrighteousness in them that perish, because they received not the love of the Truth, that they might be saved. And *for this cause* God shall send them strong delusion that they should believe a lie, that they all might be damned who believed not the Truth, but had pleasure in unrighteousness."

Hence, considering that Antichrist would pretend to be the Messiah, it was of old the received notion that he was to be of Jewish race and to observe the Jewish rites.

Further, St. Paul says that Antichrist should "sit in the Temple of God;" that is, according to the earlier Fathers, in the Jewish Temple. Our Savior's own words may be taken to support this notion, because He speaks of "the Abomination of Desolation," (which, whatever other meanings it might have, in its fullness denotes Antichrist,) "standing in the *holy place*." Further, the persecution of Christ's witnesses which Antichrist will make, is described by St. John as taking place in Jerusalem. "Their dead bodies shall lie in the street of the great city, (which spiritually is called Sodom and Egypt,) where also our Lord was crucified."

Now here a remark may be made. At first, I suppose, we

should not consider that there was much evidence from the Sacred Text for Antichrist taking part with the Jews, or having to do with their Temple. It is, then, a very remarkable fact that the apostate emperor Julian, who was a type and earnest of the great enemy, should, as he did, have taken part with the Jews, and set about building their Temple. Here the history is a sort of comment on the prophecy, and sustains and vindicates the early interpretations of it which I am relating. Of course I must be understood to mean, and a memorable circumstance it is, that this belief of the Church that Antichrist should be connected with the Jews, was expressed long before Julian's time, and that we still possess the works in which it is contained. We have the writings of two Fathers, both Bishops and martyrs of the Church, who lived at least one hundred and fifty years before Julian, and less than one hundred years after St. John. They both distinctly declare Antichrist's connection with the Jews.

The first of them, Irenaeus, speaks as follows: "In the Temple which is at Jerusalem the adversary will sit, endeavoring to show himself to be the Christ" (Iren. *Haer.*, v. 25).

And the second, Hippolytus: "Antichrist will be he who shall resuscitate the kingdom of the Jews." (Hippol. *de Antichristo*, § 25. St Cyril of Jerusalem also speaks of Antichrist building the Jewish Temple; and he too wrote before Julian's attempt, and [what is remarkable] prophesied it would fail, because of the prophecies. —*Vide* Ruff. Hist., i. 37.)

3.

Next let us ask, Will Antichrist profess any sort of religion at all? Neither true God nor false God will he worship: so far is clear, and yet something more, and that obscure, is told us. Indeed, as far as the prophetic accounts go, they seem at first sight incompatible with each other. Antichrist is to "exalt himself over all that is called God or worshipped." He will set himself forcibly against idols and idolatry, as the early teachers agree in declaring. Yet in the book of Daniel we read, "In his estate *shall he honor the god of forces; and a god whom his fathers knew not shall he honor* with gold and silver, and with precious stones and pleasant things. Thus shall he do in the most strong holds with a *strange god, whom he shall acknowledge* and increase with glory" (Dan. xi. 38, 39). What is meant by the words translated "god of forces," and afterwards called "a strange god," is quite hidden from us, and probably will be so till the event; but anyhow some sort of false worship is certainly predicted as the mark of Antichrist, with this prediction the contrary way, that he shall set himself against *all idols*, as well as against the true God. Now it is not at all extraordinary that there should be this contrariety in the prediction, for we know generally that infidelity leads to superstition, and that the men most reckless in their blasphemy are cowards also. They cannot be consistent if they would. But let me notice here again a remarkable coincidence, which is contained in the history of that type or shadow of the final apostasy which scared the world some forty or fifty years ago,—a coincidence between actual events and prophecy sufficient to show us that the apparent contradiction in the latter may easily be reconciled, though beforehand we may not see how; sufficient to remind us that the all-watchful eye, and the all-ordaining hand of God is still over the world, and that the seeds sown in prophecy above two thousand years since, are not dead, but from time to time, by blade and tender shoot, give earnest of the future harvest. Surely the world is impregnated with the elements of preternatural evil, which ever and anon, in unhealthy seasons, give lowering and muttering tokens of the wrath to come!

In that great and famous nation which is near us, once great for its love of Christ's Church, since memorable for deeds of blasphemy, which leads me here to mention it, and now, when it should be pitied and prayed for, made unhappily our own model in too many respects,—followed when it should be condemned, and admired when it should be excused,— in the capital of that powerful and celebrated nation, there took a place as we all well know, within the last fifty years, an open apostasy from Christianity; not from Christianity only, but from every kind of worship which might retain any semblance or pretence of the great truths of religion. Atheism was absolutely professed;—yet in spite of this, it seems a contradiction in terms to say it, a certain sort of worship, and that, as the prophet expresses it, "a strange worship," was introduced. Observe what this was.

I say, they avowed on the one hand Atheism. They prevailed upon a wretched man, whom their proceedings had forced upon the Church as an Archbishop, to come before them in public and declare that there was no God, and that what he had hitherto taught was a fable. They wrote up over the burial-places that death was an eternal sleep. They closed the churches, they seized and desecrated the gold and silver plate belonging to them, turning these sacred instruments, like Belshazzar, to the use of their impious revellings; they formed mock procession, clad in priestly garments, and singing profane hymns. They annulled the divine ordinance of marriage, resolving it into a mere civil contract to be made and dissolved at pleasure. These things are but part of their enormities.

On the other hand, after having broken away from all restraint towards God and man, they gave a name to the reprobate state itself into which they had thrown themselves, and exalted it, that very negation of religion, or rather that real and living blasphemy, into a kind of God. They called it LIBERTY, and they literally worshipped it as a divinity. It would almost be incredible, that men who had flung off all religion should be at the pains to assume a new and senseless worship of their own devising, whether in superstition or in mockery, were not events so recent and so notorious. After abjuring

our Lord and Saviour, and blasphemously declaring Him
to be an impostor, they proceeded to decree, in the public
assembly of the nation, the adoration of Liberty and Equality
as divinities; and they appointed festivals besides in honour
of Reason, the Country, the Constitution, and the Virtues.
Further, they determined that tutelary gods, even dead men,
may be canonized, consecrated, and worshipped; and they
enrolled in the number of these some of the most notorious
infidels and profligates of the last century. The remains of the
two principal of these were brought in solemn procession into
one of their churches, and placed upon the holy altar itself;
incense was offered to them, and the assembled multitude
bowed down in worship before one of them—before what
remained on earth of an inveterate enemy of Christ.

Now, I do not mention all this as considering it the fulfillment
of the prophecy, nor, again, as if the fulfillment when it comes
will be in this precise way, but merely to point out, what
the course of events has shown us in these latter times, that
there *are* ways of fulfilling sacred announcements that seem
at first sight contradictory,—that men may oppose every
existing worship, true and false, and yet take up a worship
of their own from pride, wantonness, policy, superstition,
fanaticism, or other reasons.

And further, let it be remarked that there was a tendency
in the infatuated people I have spoken of, to introduce the
old Roman democratic worship, as if further to show us that

Rome, the fourth monster of the prophet's vision, is not dead. They even went so far as to restore the worship of one of the Roman divinities (Ceres) by name, raised a statue to her, and appointed a festival in her honor. This indeed was inconsistent with exalting themselves "above *all* that is called god;" but I mention it, as I have said, not as throwing light upon the prophecy, but to show that the spirit of old Rome has not passed from the world, though its name is almost extinct.

Still further, it is startling to observe, that that former apostate in the early times, the Emperor Julian, he too was engaged in bringing back Roman Paganism.

Further still, let it be observed that Antiochus too, the Antichrist before Christ, the persecutor of the Jews, he too signalized himself in forcing the Pagan worship upon them, introducing it even into the Temple.

We know not what is to come; but this we may safely say, that, improbable as it is that Paganism should ever be publicly restored and enforced by authority for any time, however short, even three years and a half, yet it is far less improbable now than it was fifty years ago, before the event occurred which I have referred to. Who would not have been thought a madman or idiot before that period, who had conjectured such a portentous approximation to Paganism as actually took place?

4.

Now let us recur to the ancient Fathers, and see whether their further anticipations do not run parallel to the events which have since happened.

Antichrist, as they considered, will come out of the Roman Empire just upon its destruction;—that is, the Roman Empire will in its last days divide itself into ten parts, and the enemy will come up suddenly out of it upon these ten, and subdue three of them, or all of them perhaps, and (as the prophet continues) "shall speak great words against the Most High, and shall wear out the saints of the Most High, and think to change times and laws, and they shall be given into his hand until a time, times, and the dividing of time" (Dan. vii. 25). Now it is very observable that one of the two early Fathers whom I have already cited, Hippolytus, expressly says that the ten states which will at length appear, though kingdoms, shall also be *democracies*. I say this is observable, considering the present state of the world, the tendency of things in this day towards democracy, and the instance which has been presented to us of democracy within the last fifty years, in those occurrences in France to which I have already referred.

Another expectation of the early Church was, that the Roman monster, after remaining torpid for centuries, would wake up at the end of the world, and be restored in all its laws and forms; and this too, considering those same recent events to which I have alluded, is certainly worth noticing also. The same Father, who anticipates the coming of democracies, expressly deduces from a passage in the xiiith chapter of the Apocalypse, that "the system of Augustus, who was founder of the Roman Empire, shall be adopted and established by him (Antichrist), in order to his own aggrandizement and glory. This is the fourth monster whose head was wounded and healed; in that the empire was destroyed and came to naught, and was divided into ten diadems. But at this time Antichrist, as being an unscrupulous villain, will heal and restore it; so that it will be active and vigorous once more through the system which he establishes"(Hippol. *de Antichristo*, § 27, 49).

I will but notice one other expectation falling in with the foregoing notion of the re-establishment of Roman power, entertained by the two Fathers whom I have been quoting; viz., one concerning the name of Antichrist, as spoken of in the xiiith chapter of Revelation: "Here is wisdom," says the inspired text; "let him that hath understanding count the number of the beast, for it is the number of the man, and his number is six hundred threescore and six." Both Irenaeus and Hippolytus give a name, the letters of which together in Greek make up this number, characteristic of the position of Antichrist as the head of the Roman Empire in its restored state, viz., the word Latinus, or the Latin king.

Irenaeus speaks as follows : "Expect that the empire will first be divided into ten kings; then while they are reigning and beginning to settle and aggrandize themselves, suddenly one will come and claim the kingdom, and frighten them, having a name which contains the predicted number (666); him recognize as the Abomination of Desolation." Then he goes on to mention, together with two other words, the name of Lateinos as answering to the number, and says of it, "This is very probable, since it is the name of the last empire;—for the Latins" (that is, the Romans) "are now in power." (He adds, that he himself prefers one of the other words.)

And Hippolytus: "Since… the wound of the first monster was healed…. and it is plain that the Latins are still in power, therefore he is called the Latin King (Latinus), the name passing from an empire to an individual." (Hippol. *de Antichristo*, § 50. The Greek text seems corrupt.)

It seems then, on the whole, that, as far as the testimony of the early Church goes, Antichrist will be an open blasphemer, opposing himself to every existing worship, true and false,—a persecutor, a patron of the Jews, and a restorer of their worship, and, further, the author of a novel kind of worship. Moreover, he will appear suddenly, at the very end of the Roman empire, which once was, and now is, dormant; that he will knit it into one, and engraft his Judaism and his new worship (a sort of Paganism, it may be) upon the old discipline of Caesar Augustus ; that in consequence he will earn the title of the Latin or Roman King, as best expressive of his place and character ; lastly, that he will pass away as suddenly as he came.

5.

Now concerning this, I repeat, I do not wish to pronounce how far the early Church was right or wrong in these anticipations, though events since have variously tended to strengthen its general interpretations of Scripture prophecy.

It may be asked, What practical use is there in speaking of these things, if they be doubtful?

I answer first, that it is not unprofitable to bear in mind that we are still under what may be called a miraculous system. I do not mean to maintain that literal miracles are taking place now, but that our present state is a portion of a providential course, which began in miracle, and at least at the end of the world, if not before, will end in a miracle. The particular expectations above detailed may be right or wrong; yet an Antichrist, whoever and whatever he be, is to come ; marvels are to come ; the old Roman empire is not extinct; the devil, if bound, is bound but for a season; the contest of good and evil is not ended. I repeat it, in the present state of things, when the great object of education is supposed to be the getting rid of things supernatural, when we are bid to laugh and jeer at believing everything we do not see, are told to account for everything by things known and ascertained, and to assay every statement by the touchstone of experience, I must think that this vision of Antichrist, as a supernatural power to come, is a great providential gain, as being a counterpoise to the evil tendencies of the age.

And next, it must be profitable for our thoughts to be sent backward and forward to the beginning and the end of the Gospel times, to the first and second coming of Christ. What we want, is to *understand* that we are in the place in which the early Christians were, with the same covenant, ministry, sacraments, and duties;—to realize a state of things long past away;—to feel that we are in a sinful world, a world lying in wickedness; to discern our position in it, that we are witnesses in it, that reproach and suffering are our portion,—so that we must not "think it strange" if they come upon us, but a kind of gracious exception if they do not ; to have our hearts awake, as if we had seen Christ and His Apostles, and seen their miracles,—awake to the hope and waiting of His second coming, looking out for it, nay, desiring to see the tokens of it; thinking often and much of the judgment to come, dwelling on and adequately entering into the thought, that we individually shall be judged. All these surely are acts of true and saving faith ; and this is one substantial use of the Book of Revelation, and other prophetical parts of Scripture, quite distinct from our knowing their real interpretation, viz., to take the veil from our eyes, to lift up the covering which lies over the face of the world, and make us see day by day, as we go in and out, as we get up and lie down, as we labor, and walk, and rest, and recreate ourselves, the Throne of God set up in the midst of us, His majesty and His judgments, His Son's continual intercession for the elect, their trials, and their victory.

III

The City of Antichrist

The Angel thus interprets to St. John the vision of the Great Harlot, then enchantress, who seduced the inhabitants of the earth. He says, "The woman which thou sawest is that great city, which reigneth over the kings of the earth." The city spoken of in these words is evidently Rome, which was then the seat of empire all over the earth,—which was supreme even in Judaea. We hear of the Romans all through the Gospels and Acts. Our Saviour was born when His mother, the Blessed Virgin, and Joseph, were brought up to Bethlehem to be taxed by the Roman governor. He was crucified under Pontius Pilate, the Roman governor. St. Paul was at various times protected by the circumstance of his being a Roman citizen; on the other hand, when he was seized and imprisoned, it was by the Roman governors, and at last he was sent to Rome itself, to the emperor, and eventually martyred there, together with St. Peter. Thus the sovereignty of Rome, at the time when Christ and His Apostles preached and wrote, which is a matter of historical notoriety, is forced on our notice in the New Testament itself. It is undeniably meant by the Angel when he speaks of "the great city which reigneth over the earth."

The connection of Rome with the reign and exploits of Antichrist, is so often brought before us in the controversies of the day, that it may be well, after what I have already had occasion to say on the subject of the last enemy of the Church, to consider now what Scripture prophecy says concerning Rome; which I shall attempt to do, as before, with the guidance of the early Fathers.

1.

Now let us observe what is said concerning Rome, in the passage which the Angel concludes in the words which I have quoted, what we may deduce from it.

This great city is described under the image of a woman, cruel, profligate, and impious. She is described as arrayed in all worldly splendor and costliness, in purple and scarlet, in gold and precious stones, and pearls, as shedding and drinking the blood of the saints, till she was drunken with it. Moreover she is called by the name of "Babylon the Great," to signify her power, wealth, profaneness, pride, sensuality, and persecuting spirit, after the pattern of that former enemy of the Church. I need not here relate how all this really answered to the character and history of Rome at the time St. John spoke of it. There never was a more ambitious, haughty, hardhearted, and worldly people than the Romans; never any, for none else had ever the opportunity, which so persecuted the Church. Christians suffered ten persecutions at their hands, as they are commonly reckoned, and very horrible ones, extending over two hundred and fifty years. The day would fail to go through an account of the tortures they suffered from Rome; so that the Apostle's description was as signally fulfilled afterwards as a prophecy, as it was accurate at the time as an historical notice.

This guilty city, represented by St. John as an abandoned woman, is said to be seated on "a scarlet-colored monster, full of names of blasphemy, having seven heads and ten horns." Here we are sent back by the prophetic description to the seventh chapter of Daniel, in which the four great empires of the world are shadowed out under the figure of four beasts, a lion, a bear, a leopard, and a nameless monster, "diverse" from the rest, "dreadful and terrible and strong exceedingly;" "and it had ten horns." This surely is the very same beast which St. John saw: the ten horns mark it. Now this fourth beast in Daniel's vision is the Roman Empire; therefore "the beast," on which the woman sat, is the Roman Empire. And this agrees very accurately with the actual position of things in history; for Rome, the mistress of the world, might well be said to sit upon, and be carried about triumphantly on that world which she had subdued, and made her creature. Further, the prophet Daniel explains the ten horns of the beast to be "ten kings that shall arise" out of this Empire; in which St. John agrees, saying, "The ten horns which thou sawest are ten kings, which have received no kingdom as yet, but receive the power as kings one hour with the beast." Moreover in a former vision Daniel speaks of the Empire as destined to be "divided," as "partly strong and partly broken" (Dan. ii. 41, 42). Further still, this empire, the beast of burden of the woman, was at length to rise against her and devour her, as some savage animal might turn upon its keeper; and it was to do this in the time of its divided or multiplied existence. "The ten horns which thou sawest upon the beast, these shall hate" her, "and shall make her desolate and naked, and shall eat her flesh and burn her with fire." Such was to be the end of the great city. Lastly, three of the kings, perhaps all, are said to be subdued by Antichrist, who is to come up suddenly while they are in power; for such is the course of Daniel's prophecy: "Another shall rise after them, and he shall be diverse from the fist, and he shall subdue three kings, and he shall speak great words against the Most High, and shall wear out the saints of the Most High, and think to change times and laws; and they shall be given into his hands until a time, times, and the dividing of time." This power, who was to rise upon the kings, is Antichrist; and I would have you observe how Rome and Antichrist stand towards each other in the prophecy. Rome is to fall before Antichrist rises; for the ten kings are to destroy Rome, and Antichrist is then to appear and supersede the ten kings. As far as we dare judge from the words, this seems clear. St. John says, "The ten horns shall hate and devour" the woman: and Daniel says, "I considered the horns, and behold, there came up among them another little horn," viz., Antichrist, "before whom" or by whom "there were three of the first horns plucked up by the roots."

2.

Now then, let us consider how far these prophecies have been fulfilled, and what seems to remain unfulfilled.

In the first place, the Roman Empire did break up, as foretold. It divided into a number of separate kingdoms, such as our own, France, and the like; yet it is difficult to number ten accurately and exactly. Next, though Rome certainly has been desolated in the most fearful and miserable way, yet it has not exactly suffered from ten parts of its own former empire, but from barbarians who came down upon it from regions external to it; and, in the third place, it still exists as a city, whereas it was to be "desolated, devoured, and burned with fire." Fourthly, there is one point in the description of the ungodly city, which has hardly been fulfilled at all in the case of Rome. She had "a golden cup in her hand full of abominations," and made "the inhabitants of the earth drunk with the wine of her fornication;" expressions which imply surely some seduction or delusion which she was enabled to practice upon the world, and which, I say, has not been fulfilled in the case of that great imperial city upon seven hills of which St. John spoke. Here then are points which require some consideration.

I say, the Roman empire has scarcely yet been divided into ten. The prophet Daniel is conspicuous among the inspired writers for the clearness and exactness of his predictions; so much so, that some unbelievers, overcome by the truth of them, could only take refuge in the unworthy, and, at the same time, unreasonable and untenable supposition, that they were written after the events which they profess to foretell. But we have had no such exact fulfillment in history of the ten kings; therefore we must suppose that it is yet to come. With this accords the ancient notion, that they were to come at the end of the world, and last but a short time, Antichrist, coming upon them. There have, indeed, been approximations to that number, yet I conceive, nothing more. Now observe how the actual state of things corresponds to the prophecy, and to the primitive interpretation of it. It is difficult to say whether the Roman Empire is gone or not; in one sense, it is gone, for it is divided into kingdoms; in another sense it is not, for the date cannot be assigned at which it came to an end, and much might be said in various ways to show that it might be considered still existing, though in a mutilated and decayed state. But if this be so, and if it is to end in ten vigorous kings, as Daniel says, then it must one day *revive*. Now observe, I say, how the prophetic description answers to this account of it. "The wild Beast," that is, the Roman Empire, "the Monster that thou sawest, *was and is not*, and *shall* ascend out of the abyss, and go into perdition." Again, mention is made of "the Beast that was, and *is not, and yet is.*" Again, we are expressly told that the ten kings and the Empire shall rise together; the kings appearing at the time of the monster's resurrection, not in its languid and torpid state. "The ten kings... have received no kingdom as yet, but receive power as kings one hour with the beast." If, then, the Roman Empire is still prostrate, the ten kings have not come; and if the ten kings have not come, the destined destroyers of the woman, the full judgments upon Rome have not yet come.

3.

Thus the full measure of judgment has not fallen up Rome; yet her sufferings, and the sufferings of her empire, have been very severe. St. Peter seems to predict them, in his First Epistle, as then impending. He seems to imply that our Lord's visitation, which was then just occurring, was no local or momentary vengeance upon one people or city, but a solemn and extended judgment of the whole earth, though beginning at Jerusalem. "The time is come," he says, "when judgment must begin at *the house* of God" (at the sacred city); "and, if it first begin at us, what shall the end be of them that obey not the Gospel of God? And if the righteous scarcely be saved,"— (*i.e.*, the remnant who should go forth of Zion, according to the prophecy, that chosen seed in the Jewish Church which received Christ when He came, and took the new name of Christians, and shot forth and grew far and wide into a fresh Church, or, in other words, the elect whom our Saviour speaks of as being involved in all the troubles and judgments of the devoted people, yet safely carried through); "if the righteous scarcely be saved, where shall the ungodly and the sinner appear,"—the inhabitants of the world at large? (1 Pet. iv. 17,18. *Vide* also Jer. xxv. 28, 29. Ezek. ix. 6.)

Here is intimation of the presence of a fearful scourge, which was then going over all the ungodly world, beginning at apostate Jerusalem, and punishing it. Such was the case: vengeance first fell upon the once holy city, which was destroyed by the Romans: it proceeded next against the executioners themselves. (*Vide* Is. xlvii. 5,6.) The empire was disorganized, and broken to pieces by dissensions and insurrections, by plagues, famines, and earthquakes, while countless hosts of barbarians attacked it from the north and east, and portioned it out, and burned and pillaged Rome itself. The judgment, I say, which began at Jerusalem, steadily tracked its way for centuries round and round the world, till at length, with unerring aim, it smote, the haughty mistress of all nations herself, the guilty woman seated upon the fourth monster which Daniel saw. I will mention one or two of these fearful inflictions.

Hosts of barbarians came down upon the civilized world, the Roman empire. One multitude,—though multitude is a feeble word to describe them,—invaded France, (A.D. 407. *Vide* Gibbon, *Hist.*, vol. v. chap 30) which was living in peace and prosperity under the shadow of Rome. They desolated and burned town and country. Seventeen provinces were made a desert. Eight metropolitan cities were set on fire and destroyed. Multitudes of Christians perished even in the churches.

The fertile coast of Africa was the scene of another of these invasions (A.D. 430. *Vide* Gibbon, *Hist.*, vol. vi. chap. 33). The barbarians gave no quarter to any who opposed them. They tortured their captives, of whatever age, rank and sex, to force them to discover their wealth. They drove away inhabitants of the cities to the mountains. They ransacked the churches. They destroyed even the fruit-trees, so complete was the desolation.

Of judgments in the course of nature, I will mention three out of a great number. One, an inundation from the sea in all parts of the Eastern empire. The water overflowed the coast for two miles inland, sweeping away houses and inhabitants along a line of some thousand miles. One great city (Alexandria) lost fifty thousand persons (A.D. 365. *Ibid.*, vol. iv. Chap 26).

The second, a series of earthquakes; some of which were felt all over the empire. Constantinople was thus shaken above forty days together. At Antioch 250,000 persons perished in another.

And in the third place a plague, which lasted (languishing and reviving) through the long period of fifty-two years. In

Constantinople during three months there died daily 5000, and at length 10,000 persons. I give these facts from a modern writer, who is neither favorable to Christianity, nor credulous in matters of historical testimony. In some countries the population was wasted away altogether, and has not recovered to this day (A.D. 540. *Ibid.*, vol. vii. Chap 43).

Such were the scourges by which the fourth monster of Daniel's vision was brought low, "the Lord God's sore judgments, the sword, the famine, and the pestilence (Ezek. xiv. 21). Such was the process by which "that which withholdeth," (in St. Paul's language) began to be "taken away;" though not altogether removed even now.

And, while the world itself was thus plagued, not less was the offending city which had ruled it. Rome was taken and plundered three several times. The inhabitants were murdered, made captives, or obliged to fly all over Italy. The gold and jewels of the queen of the nations, her precious silk and purple, and her works of art, were carried off or destroyed.

4.

These are great and notable events, and certainly form part of the predicted judgment upon Rome; at the same time they do not adequately fulfill the prophecy, which says expressly, on the one hand, that the ten portions of the Empire itself which had almost been slain, shall rise up against the city, and "make her desolate and burn her with fire," which they have not yet done; and, on the other hand, that the city shall experience a *total* destruction, which has not yet befallen her, for she still exists. St. John's words on the latter point are clear and determinate. "Babylon the great is fallen, is fallen; and is become the habitation of devils, and the hole of every foul spirit, and a cage of every unclean and hateful bird;" (Ezek . xiv. 21) words which would seem to refer us to the curse upon the literal Babylon; and we know how it was fulfilled. The prophet Isaiah had said, that in Babylon "wild beasts of the desert should lie there, and their houses be full of doleful creatures, and owls should dwell there, and satyrs," or devils, "should dance there" (Isa. xiii. 21). And we know that all this has happened to Babylon; it is a heap of ruin; no man dwells there; nay, it is difficult to say even where exactly it was placed, so great is the desolation. Such a desolation St. John seems to predict, concerning the guilty persecuting city we are considering; and in spite of what she has suffered, such a desolation has not come upon her yet. Again, "she shall be utterly burnt with fire, for strong is the Lord God, who judgeth her." Surely this implies utter destruction, annihilation. Again, "a mighty Angel took up a stone, like a great millstone, and cast it into the sea, saying, Thus with violence shall that great city Babylon be thrown down, and *shall be found no more at all*."

To these passages I would add this reflection. Surely Rome is spoken of in Scripture as a more inveterate enemy of God and His saints even than Babylon, as the great pollution and bane of the earth: if then Babylon has been destroyed wholly, much more, according to all reasonable conjecture, will Rome be destroyed one day.

It may be farther observed, that serious men in the early Church certainly thought that the barbarian invasions were not all that Rome was to receive in the way of vengeance, but that God would one day destroy it by the fury of the elements. "Rome," says Pope Gregory, at a time when a barbarian conqueror had possession of the city, and all things seemed to threaten its destruction, "Rome shall not be destroyed by the nations, but shall consume away internally, worn out by storms of lightning, whirlwinds, and earthquakes" (Greg. *Dial.*, ii. 15). In accordance with this is the prophecy ascribed to St. Malachi of Armagh, a medieval Archbishop (A.D. 1130), which declares, "In the last persecution of the Holy Church, Peter of Rome shall be on the throne, who shall feed his flock in many tribulations. When these are past, *the city upon seven hills shall be* destroyed and the awful Judge shall judge the people" (*Vide* Dr. Burton, *Antiq. of Rome,* p. 475).

5.

This is what may be said on the one side, but after all something may be said on the other; not indeed to show that the prophecy is already fully accomplished, for it certainly is not, but to show that, granting this, such accomplishment as has to come has reference, not to Rome, but to some other object or objects of divine vengeance. I shall explain my meaning under two heads.

First, why has not Rome been destroyed hitherto? How was it that the barbarians left it? Babylon sunk under the avenger whom God brought against it—Rome has not: why is this? for if there has been a something to procrastinate the vengeance due to Rome hitherto, peradventure that obstacle may act again and again, and stay the uplifted hand of divine wrath till the end come. The cause of this unexpected respite seems to be simply this, that when the barbarians came down, God had a people in that city. Babylon was a mere prison of the Church; Rome had received her as a guest. The Church dwelt in Rome, and while her children suffered in the heathen city from the barbarians, so again they were there the life and the salt of the city where they suffered.

Christians understood this at the time, and availed themselves of their position. They remembered Abraham's intercession for Sodom, and the gracious announcement made him, that had there been ten righteous men therein, it would have been saved.

When the city was worsted, threatened, and at length overthrown, the Pagans had cried out that Christianity was the cause of this. They said they had always flourished under their idols, and that these idols and devils (gods as they called them) were displeased at them for the numbers among them who had been converted to the faith of the Gospel, and had in consequence deserted them, given them over to their enemies, and brought vengeance upon them. On the other hand, they scoffed at the Christians, saying in effect, "Where is now your God? Why does he not save you? You are not better off than we;" they said, with the impenitent thief, "If Thou be the Christ, save Thyself and us;" or, with the multitude, "If He be the Son of God, let him come down from the Cross." This was during the time of one of the most celebrated bishops and doctors of the Church, St. Augustine; and he replied to their challenge. He replied to them, and to his brethren also, some of whom were offended and shocked that such calamities should have happened to a city which had become Christian (August., *de Urbis Excidio*, vol. vi. p. 622, ed. Ben. and *de Civ. Dei* i. 1-7). He pointed to the cities which had already sinned and been visited, and showed that they had altogether perished, whereas Rome was still preserved. Here then he said was the very fulfillment of the promise of God, announced to Abraham; for the sake of the Christians in it, Rome was chastised, not overthrown utterly.

Historical facts support St. Augustine's view of things: God provided visibly, not only in His secret counsels, that the Church should be the salvation of the city. The fierce conqueror Alaric, who first came against it, exhorted his troops, "to respect the Churches of the Apostles St. Peter and St. Paul, as holy and inviolable sanctuaries;" and he gave orders that a quantity of plate consecrated to St. Peter should be removed into his Church from the place where it had been discovered (*Vide* Gibbon, *Hist.*, vol. v. chap. 31).

Again, fifty years afterwards, when Attila was advancing against the city, the Bishop of Rome of the day, St. Leo, formed one of a deputation of three, who went out to meet him, and was successful in arresting his purpose.

A few years afterwards, Genseric, the most savage of the barbarian conquerors, appeared before the defenseless city. The same fearless pontiff went out to meet him at the head of the clergy, and though he did not succeed in saving the city from pillage, yet he gained a promise that the unresisting multitude should be spared, the buildings protected from fire, and the captives from torture (*Ibid.* vol. vi. chap. 35, 36).

Thus from the Goth, Hun, and Vandal, did the Christian Church shield the guilty city in which she dwelt. What a wonderful rule of God's providence is herein displayed, which occurs daily!—the Church sanctifies, yet suffers with the world, sharing its sufferings yet lightening them. In the case before us, she has (if we may humbly say it) suspended, to this day, the vengeance destined to fall upon the city which was drunk with the blood of the martyrs of Jesus.

That vengeance has never fallen; it is still suspended; nor can reason be given *why* Rome has not fallen under the rule of God's general dealings with His rebellious creatures, and suffered (according to the prophecy), the fullness of God's wrath begun in it, except that a Christian Church is still in that city, sanctifying it, interceding for it, saving it. We in England consider that the Christian Church there has in process of time become infected with the sins of Rome itself, and learned to be ambitious and cruel after the fashion of those who possessed the place aforetimes. Yet, if it were what many would make it, if it were as reprobate as heathen Rome itself, what stays the judgment long ago begun? why does not the Avenging Arm, which made its first stroke ages since, deal its second and its third, till the city has fallen? Why is not Rome as Sodom and Gomorrah, if there be righteous men in it?

This then is the first remark I would make as to the fulfillment of the prophecy which is not yet come; perhaps through divine mercy, it may be procrastinated even to the end, and never be fulfilled. Of this we can know nothing one way or the other.

Secondly, let it be considered, that as Babylon is a type of Rome, and of the world of sin an vanity, so Rome in turn may be a type also, whether of some other city, or of a proud and deceiving world. The woman is said to be Babylon as well as Rome, and as she is something more than Babylon, namely, Rome, so again she may be something more than Rome, which is yet to come. Various great cities in Scripture, are made, in their ungodliness and ruin, types of the world itself. Their end is described in figures which in their fullness apply only to the end of the world; the sun and moon are said to fall, the earth to quake, and the stars to fall from heaven (*Vide* Isaiah xiii. 10, etc.). The destruction of Jerusalem in our Lord's prophecy is associated with the end of all things. As then their ruin prefigures a greater and wider judgment, so the chapters, on which I have been dwelling, may have a further accomplishment, not in Rome, but in the world itself, or some other great city to which we cannot at present apply them, or to all the great cities of the world together, and to the spirit that rules in them, their avaricious, luxurious, self-dependent, irreligious spirit. And in this sense is already fulfilled a portion of the chapter before us, which does not apply to heathen Rome;—I mean the description of the woman as making men drunk with her sorceries and delusions; for such, surely, nothing else than an intoxication, is that arrogant, ungodly, falsely liberal, and worldly spirit, which great cities make dominant in a country.

6.

To sum up what I have said. The question asked was, Is it not true (as is commonly said and believed among us) that Rome is mentioned in the Apocalypse, as having especial share in the events which will come at the end of the world by means, or after the time, of Antichrist? I answer this, that Rome's judgments have come on her in great measure, when her Empire was taken from her; that her persecutions of the Church have been in great measure avenged, and the Scripture predictions concerning her fulfilled; that whether or not she shall be further judged depends on two circumstances, first, whether "the righteous men" in the city who saved her when her judgment first came, will not, through God's great mercy, be allowed to save her still; next, whether the prophecy relates in its fullness to Rome or to some other object or objects of which Rome is a type. And further, I say, that if it is in the divine counsels that Rome should still be judged, this must be before Antichrist comes, because Antichrist comes upon and destroys the ten kings, and lasts but a short space, but it is the ten kings who are to destroy Rome. On the other hand, so far would seem to be clear, that the prophecy itself has not been fully accomplished, whatever we decide about Rome's concern in it. The Roman empire has not yet been divided into ten heads, nor has it yet risen against the woman, whomsoever she stands for, nor has the woman yet received her ultimate judgment.

We are warned against sharing in her sins, and in her punishment;—against being found when the end comes, mere children of this world and of its great cities; with tastes, opinions, habits, such as are found in its cities; with a heart dependent on human society, and a reason molded by it;—against finding ourselves at the last day, before our Judge, with all the low feelings, principles, and aims which the world encourages; with our thoughts wandering (if that be possible then), wandering after vanities; with thoughts which rise no higher than the consideration of our own comforts, of our gains; with a haughty contempt for the Church, her ministers, her lowly people; a love of rank and station, an admiration of the splendor and the fashions of the world, an affectation of refinement, a dependence upon our powers of reason, an habitual self-esteem, and an utter ignorance of the number and the heinousness of the sins which lie against us. If we are found thus, when the end comes, where, when the judgment is over, and the saints have gone up to heaven, and there is silence and darkness where all was so full of life and expectation, where shall we find ourselves then? And what good could the great Babylon do us then, though it were as immortal as we are immortal ourselves?

IV

The Persecution of Antichrist

We have been so accustomed to hear of the persecutions of the Church, both from the New Testament and from the history of Christianity, that it is well if we have not at length come to regard the account of them as words of course, to speak of them without understanding what we say, and to receive no practical benefit from having been told of them: much less are we likely to take them for what they really are, a characteristic mark of Christ's Church. They are not indeed the necessary lot of the Church, but at least one of her appropriate badges; so that on the whole, looking at the course of history, you might set down persecution as one of the peculiarities by which you recognize her. And our Lord seems to intimate how becoming, how natural persecution is to the Church, by placing it among His Beatitudes. "Blessed are they who are persecuted for righteousness' sake, for theirs is the kingdom of heaven;" giving it the same high and honorable rank in the assemblage of evangelical graces, which the Sabbath holds among the ten Commandments,—I mean, as a sort of sign and token of His followers, and, as such, placed in the moral code, though in itself external to it.

He seems to show us this in another way, viz., as intimating to us the fact, that in persecution the Church beings and in persecution she ends. He left her in persecution, and He will find her in persecution. He recognizes her as His own,—He framed, and He will claim her,—as a persecuted Church, bearing His Cross. And that awful relic of Him which He gave her, and which she is found with at the end, she cannot have lost by the way.

The prophet Daniel, who shadows out for us so many things about the last time, speaks of the great persecution yet to come. He says, "There shall be a time of trouble, such as never was since there was a nation even to that same time; and at that time thy people shall be delivered, every one that shall be found written in the Book." To these words our Lord seems to refer, in His solemn prophecy before His passion, in which He comprises both series of events, both those which attended His first, and those which will attend at His second coming—both persecutions of His Church, the early and the late. He speaks as follows: "Then shall be great tribulation, such as was not since the beginning of the world to this time, no, nor ever shall be; and except those days should be shortened, there should no flesh be saved; but for the elect's sake, those days shall be shortened" (Matt. xxiv. 21,22).

Now I shall conclude what I have to say about the coming of Antichrist by speaking of the persecution which will attend it. In saying that a persecution will attend it, I do but speak the opinion of the early Church, as I have tried to do all along, and shall do in what follows.

1.

First, I will cite some of the principal texts which seem to refer to this last persecution.

"Another shall rise after them and… he shall speak great words against the Most High, and shall wear out the saints of the most High, and think to change times and laws; and they shall be given into his hand until a time, times, and the dividing of time;" (Dan. vii. 24,25) that is, three years and a half.

"They shall pollute the Sanctuary of strength, and shall take away the Daily Sacrifice, and they shall place the Abomination that maketh desolate, and such as do wickedly against the Covenant shall he corrupt by flatteries; but the people that do know their God shall be strong and do exploits. And they that understand among the people, shall instruct many; yet they shall fall by the sword, and by flame, by captivity, and by spoil, many days" (Dan. xi. 31-33).

"Many shall be purified, and made white, and tried; but the wicked shall do wickedly;… and from the time that the Daily Sacrifice shall be taken away, and the Abomination that maketh desolate set up, there shall be a thousand two hundred and ninety days" (Dan. xii. 10,11).

"Then shall be great tribulation, such as was not since the beginning of the world," (Matt. xxiv. 21) and so on; as I just now read it.

"And there was given unto him a mouth speaking great things and blasphemies; and power was given unto him to continue forty and two months. And he opened his mouth in blasphemy against God, to blaspheme His name, and His tabernacle, and them that dwell in heaven: and it was given unto him to make war with the saints, and to overcome them… and all that dwell upon the earth shall worship him, whose names are not written in the book of life of the Lamb slain from the foundation of the world" (Rev. xiii. 5-8).

"I saw an Angel come down from heaven, having the key of the bottomless pit, and a great chain in his hand; and he laid hold on the dragon, that old serpent, which is the devil and Satan, and bound him a thousand years… and after that he must be loosed a little season… and shall go out to deceive the nations which are in the four quarters of the earth, Gog and Magog, to gather them together to battle: the number of whom is as the sand of the sea. And they went up on the breadth of the earth, and compassed the camp of the saints about, and the beloved city" (Rev. xx. 1-9).

These passages were understood by the early Christians to relate to the persecution, which was to come in the last times; and they seem, evidently to bear upon them that meaning. Our Lord's words, indeed, about the fierce trial which was coming, might seem at first sight to refer to the early persecutions, those to which the first Christians were exposed; and doubtless so they do also: yet, violent as these persecutions were, they were not considered by those who suffered them to be the proper fulfillment of the prophecy; and this surely is itself a strong reason for thinking they were not so. And we are confirmed by parallel passages, such as the words of Daniel, quoted just now, which certainly speak of a persecution still future; if then our Lord used those very words of Daniel, and was speaking of what Daniel spoke of, therefore, whatever partial accomplishment His prediction had in the early Church, He surely speaks of nothing short of the last persecution, when His words are viewed in their full scope. He says, "There shall be great tribulation, such as was not since the beginning of the world to this time, no, nor ever shall be: and except those days should be shortened, there shall no flesh be saved; but for the elect's sake those days shall be shortened." And immediately after, "There shall arise false Christs and false prophets, and shall show great signs of wonders; insomuch that, if it were possible, they shall deceive the very elect." In accordance with this language, Daniel says, "There shall be a time of trouble, such as never was since there was a nation, even to that same time: and at that time thy people shall be delivered, every one that shall be found written in the book." One of the passages I quoted from the Revelation says the same, and as strongly: "It was given him to make war with the Saints, and to overcome them... and all that dwell on the earth shall worship him, whose names are not written in the book of life" (Rev. xiii. 7,8).

2.

Let us then apprehend and realize the idea, thus clearly brought before us, that, sheltered as the Church has been from persecution for 1500 years, yet a persecution awaits it, before the end, fiercer and more perilous than any which occurred at its first rise.

Further, this persecution is to be attended with the cessation of all religious worship. "They shall take away the Daily Sacrifice,"—words which the early Fathers interpret to mean, that Antichrist will suppress for three years and a half all religious worship. St. Augustine questions whether baptism even will be administered to infants during that season.

And further, we are told: "They shall place the Abomination that maketh desolate" in the Holy Place—they shall "set it up:" our Savior declares the same. What this means we cannot pronounce. In the former fulfillment of this prophecy, it has been the introduction of heathen idols into God's house.

Moreover the reign of Antichrist will be supported, it would appear, with a display of miracles, such as the magicians of Egypt effected against Moses. On this subject, of course, we wait for a fuller explanation of the prophetical language, such as the event alone can give us. So far, however, is clear, that whether false miracles or not, whether pretended, or the result, as some have conjectured, of discoveries in physical science, they will produce the same effect as if they were real,—viz. the overpowering the imaginations of such as have not the love of God deeply lodged in their hearts,— of all but the elect. Scripture is remarkably precise and consistent in this prediction. "Signs and wonders," says our Lord, "insomuch that, if it were possible, they shall deceive the very elect." St. Paul speaks of Antichrist as one "whose coming is after the working of Satan, with all powers and signs, and lying wonders, and with all deceivableness of unrighteousness in them that perish; because they received not the love of the Truth, that they might be saved. And for this cause God shall send them strong delusion, that they should believe a lie" (2 Thess. ii. 9-11). And St. John: "He doeth great wonders so that He maketh fire come down from heaven on the earth in the sight of men, and deceiveth them that dwell on the earth by the means of those miracles which he had power to do in sight of the beast" (Rev. xiii. 13,14).

In these four respects, then, not to look for others, will the last persecution be more awful than any of the earlier ones: in its being in itself fiercer and more horrible; in its being attended by a cessation of the ordinances of grace, "the Daily Sacrifice;" and by an open and blasphemous establishment of infidelity, or some such enormity, in the holiest recess of the Church; lastly, in being supported by a power of working miracles. Well is it for Christians that the days are shortened!—shortened for the elect's sake, lest they should be overwhelmed,—shortened, as it would seem, to three years and a half.

3.

Much might be said, of course, on each of these four particulars; but I will confine myself to making one remark on the first of them, the sharpness of the persecution.—It is to be worse than any persecution before it. Now, to understand the force of the announcement, we should understand in some degree what those former persecutions were.

This it is very difficult to do in a few words; yet a very slight survey of the history of the Church will convince as that cruelties more shocking than those which the early Christians suffered from their persecutors, it is very difficult to conceive. St. Paul's words, speaking of the persecutions prior to his time, but faintly describe the trial which came upon the Church in his day and afterwards. He says of the Jewish saints, "They were tortured, not accepting deliverance"... they "had trials of cruel mocking and scourging, yea, moreover, of bonds and imprisonment: they

68

were stoned, they were sawn asunder, were tempted, were slain with the sword: they wandered about in sheepskins and goatskins; being destitute, afflicted, tormented." Such were the trials of the Prophets under the Law, who in a measure anticipated the Gospel, as in creed, so in suffering; yet the Gospel suffering was as much sharper, as the Gospel creed was fuller than their foretaste of either.

Let me take, as a single specimen, a portion of a letter, giving an account of some details of one of the persecutions in the south of France. It is written by eye-witnesses:

". . . The rage of the populace, governor, and soldiers, especially lighted on Sanctus, a deacon; on Maturus, a late convert; on Attalus, and on Blandina, a slave, through whom Christ showed that the things which are lowly esteemed among men, have high account with God. For when we were all in fear, and her own mistress was in agony for her, lest she should be unable to make even one bold confession, from the weakness of her body, Blandina was filled with such strength, that even those who tortured her by turns, in every possible way, from morning till evening, were wearied and gave it up, confessing she had conquered them. And they wondered at her remaining still alive, her whole body being mangled and pierced in every part. But that blessed woman, like a brave combatant, renewed her strength in confessing; and it was to her a recovery, a rest, and a respite, to say, 'I am a Christian.' ... Sanctus also endured exceedingly all the cruelties of men with a noble patience… and to all questions would say nothing but 'I am a Christian.' When they had nothing left to do to him, they fastened red hot plates of brass on the tenderest parts of his body. But though his limbs were burning, he remained upright and unshrinking, steadfast in his confession, bathed and strengthened from Heaven with that fountain of living water that springs from the well of Christ. But his body bore witness of what had been done to it, being one entire wound and deprived of the external form of man."

After some days they were taken to the shows where the wild beasts were, and went through every torture again, as though they had suffered nothing before. Again they were scourged, forced into the iron chair (which was red hot), dragged about by the beasts, and so came to their end. "But Blandina was hung upon a cross, and placed to be devoured by the beasts that were turned in." Afterwards she was scourged; at last placed in a basket and thrown to a bull, and died under the tossings of the furious animal. But the account is far too long and minute, and too dreadful, to allow of my going through it. I give this merely as a specimen of the sufferings of the early Christians from the malice of the devil.

As another instance, take again the sufferings which the Arian Vandals inflicted at a later time. Out of four hundred and sixty Bishops in Africa, they sent forty-six out of the country to an unhealthy place, and confined them to hard labor, and three hundred and two to different parts of Africa. After an interval of ten years, they banished two hundred and twenty more. At another time they tore above four thousand Christians, clergy and laity, from their homes, and marched them across the sands, till they died either of fatigue or ill-usage. They lacerated others with scourges, burned them with hot iron, and cut off their limbs (Gibbon, *Hist.*, chap. 37).

Hear how one of the early Fathers, just when the early persecutions were ceasing, meditates on the prospect lying before the Church, looking earnestly at the events of his own day, in order to discover from them, if he could, whether the predicted evil was coming:

"There will be a time of affliction, such as never happened since there was a nation upon the earth till that time. The fearful monster, the great serpent, the unconquerable enemy of mankind, ready to devour.... The Lord, knowing the greatness of the enemy, in mercy to the religious, says 'Let those that are in Judaea flee to the mountains.' However, if any feel within him a strong heart to wrestle with Satan, let him remain (for I do not despair of the Church's strength of nerve,) let him remain, and let him say, 'Who shall separate us from the love of Christ?' ... Thanks to God, who limits the greatness of the affliction to a few days, 'for the elect's sake those days shall be cut short.' ... Antichrist shall reign only three years and a half," a time, times, and the dividing of times… Blessed surely he who then shall be a martyr for Christ! I consider that the martyrs at that season will be greater than all martyrs; for the former ones wrestled with man only; but these, in the time of Antichrist, will battle with Satan himself personally. Persecuting emperors slaughtered the former; but they did not pretend to raise the dead, nor make show of signs and wonders: but here there will be the persuasion both of force and of fraud, so as to deceive, if possible, even the elect. Let no one at that day say in his heart, 'What could Christ do more than this? by what virtue worketh he these things? Unless God willed it, He would not have permitted it.' No: The Apostle forewarns you, saying beforehand, 'God shall send there a strong delusion,'—not that they may be excused, but condemned— viz. who believe not in the Truth, that is, the true Christ, but take pleasure in unrighteousness, that is, in Antichrist…. Prepare thyself, therefore, O man! thou hearest the signs of Antichrist; nor remind only thyself of them, but communicate them liberally to all around thee. If thou hast a child according to the flesh, delay not to instruct him. If thou art a teacher, prepare also thy spiritual children, lest they take the false for the True. 'For the mystery of iniquity doth already work.' I fear the wars of the nations; I fear the divisions among Christians; I fear the hatred among brethren. Enough; but God forbid that it should be fulfilled in our day. However, let us be prepared" (*Cyr. Catech.*, xv. 16,17).

4.

I have two remarks to add: first, that it is quite certain, that if such a persecution has been foretold, it has not yet come, and therefore is to come. We may be wrong in thinking that Scripture foretells it, though it has been the common belief, I may say, of all ages; but if there be a persecution, it is still future. So that every generation of Christians should be on the watch-tower, looking out,—nay, more and more, as time goes on.

Next, I observe that signs do occur from time to time, not to enable us to fix the day, for that is hidden, but to show us it is coming. The world grows old—the earth is crumbling away—the night is far spent—the day is at hand. The shadows begin to move—the old forms of empire which have lasted ever since our Lord was with us, heave and tremble before our eyes, and nod to their fall. These it is that keep Him from us—He is behind them. When they go, Antichrist will be released from "that which withholdeth," and after his short but fearful season Christ will come.

For instance: one sign is the present state of the Roman Empire, if it may be said to exist, though it does exist; but it is like a man on his death-bed, who after many throes and pangs, at last goes off when you least expect, or perhaps you know not when. You watch the sick man, and you say every day will be the last; yet day after day goes on—you know not when the end will come—he lingers on—gets better—relapses,—yet you are sure after all he must die—it is a mere matter of time, you call it a matter of time: so is it with the Old Roman Empire, which now lies so still and helpless. It is not dead, but it is on its death-bed. We suppose indeed that it will not die without some violence even yet, without convulsions. Antichrist is to head it; yet in another sense it dies to make way for Antichrist, and this latter form of death is surely hastening on, whether it comes sooner or later. It may outlast our time, and the time of our children; for we are creatures of a day, and a generation is like the striking of a clock; but it tends to dissolution, and its hours are numbered.

Again, another anxious sign at the present time is what appears in the approaching destruction of the Mahometan power. This too may outlive our day; still it tends visibly to annihilation, and as it crumbles, perchance the sands of the world's life are running out.

And lastly, not to mention many other tokens which might be observed upon, here is this remarkable one. In one of the passages I just now read from the book of Revelation, it is said that in the last times, and in order to the last persecution, Satan, being loosed from his prison, shall deceive the nations in the extremities of the earth, Gog and Magog, and bring them to battle against the Church. These appellations had been already used by the prophet Ezekiel, who borrows the latter of them from the tenth chapter of

Genesis. We read in that chapter that after the flood the sons of Japheth were "Gomer, and Magog, and Madai, and Javan, and Tubal, and Meshech, and Tiras." Magog is supposed to be the ancestor of the nations in the north, the Tartars or Scythians. Whatever then Gog means, which is not known, here is a prophecy that the northern nations should be stirred up against the Church, and be one of the instruments of its suffering. And it is to be observed that twice since that prophecy was delivered, the northern nations have invaded the Church, and both times they have brought with them, or rather (as the text in the Revelations expresses it) they have been deceived into, an Antichristian delusion,—been deceived into it, not invented it. The first irruption was that of the Goths and Vandals in the early times of the Church, and they were deceived into and fought for the Arian heresy. The next was that of the Turks, and they in like manner were deceived into and fought for Mahometanism. Here then the after history, as in other instances, is in part of comment upon the prophecy. Now, I do not mean that as to the present time, we see how this is to be accomplished in its fullness, after the pattern of the Shadows which have gone before. But thus much we see—we see that in matter of fact the nations of the North [e.g., The Chinese?] are gathering strength, and beginning to frown over the seat of the Roman Empire as they never have done since the time when the Turks came down. Here then we have a sign of Antichrist's appearance—I do not say of his instant coming, or his certain coming, for it may after all be but a type or shadow of things far future; still, so far as it goes, it is a preparation, a warning, a call to sober thought—just as a cloud in the sky (to use our Lord's instance) warns us about the weather. It is no sure proof that it precedes a storm, but we think it prudent to keep our eye upon it.

5.

This is what I have to say about the last persecution and its signs. And surely it is profitable to think about it, though we be quite mistaken in the detail. For instance, after all perhaps it may not be a persecution of blood and death, but of craft and subtlety only—not of miracles, but of natural wonders and powers of human skill, human acquirements in the hands of the devil. Satan may adopt the more alarming weapons of deceit—he may hide himself—he may attempt to seduce us in little things, and so to move the Christians, not all at once, but by little and little from their true position. We know he has done much in this way in the course of the last few centuries. It is his policy to split us up and divide us, to dislodge us gradually from off our rock of strength. And if there is to be a persecution, perhaps it will be then; then, perhaps, when we are all of us in all parts of Christendom so divided, and so reduced, so full of schism, so close upon heresy. When we have cast ourselves upon the world and depend for protection upon it, and have given up our independence and our strength, then he may burst upon us in fury as far as God allows him. Then suddenly the Roman Empire may break up, and Antichrist appear as a persecutor, and the barbarous nations around break in. But all these things are in God's hand and God's knowledge, and there let us leave them.

This alone I will say, in conclusion, as I have already said several times, that such meditations as these may be turned to good account. It will act as a curb upon our self-willed, selfish hearts, to believe that a persecution is in store for the Church, whether or not it comes in our days! Surely with this prospect before us we cannot bear to give ourselves up to thoughts of ease and comfort, of making money, settling well, or rising in the world. Surely with this prospect before us, we cannot but feel that we are, what all Christians really are in the best estate (nay, rather would wish to be, had they their will, if they be Christians in heart), *pilgrims*, watchers waiting for the morning, waiting for the light, eagerly straining our eyes for the first dawn of day—looking out for our Lord's coming. His glorious advent, when He will end the reign of sin and wickedness, accomplish the number of His elect, and perfect those who at present struggle with infirmity, yet in their hearts love and obey Him.

More Titles from Roman Catholic Books

The Catholic Bible in Pictures, *Msgr. Dante Del Fiorentino* (editor). Magnificent Bible picture book includes EVERY significant story in the Bible (both Testaments), told in sequences of three to ten captioned pictures. 1,085 pen-and-ink illustrations by 11 talented artists. Special full-color section. Index of Biblical names and places. Hardcover, $29.95

Neuroses and Sacraments, *Fr. Alan Keenan*. How neurotics can live good Catholic lives, despite struggles and pain. Written by a well-known Franciscan preacher of the mid-20th century. Hardcover, $20.95

Reflections on Growing Old, *Fr. Bede Jarrett, O.P.* How to conquer your fear of aging—and make your senior years your best. Hardcover, $21.80

The Roots of Violence, *Rev. Vincent P. Miceli, S.J.* The roots of violence are hatred of God's created order and a refusal to serve Him, shows Father Miceli in this 1980s book, which is especially topical today. Appendix: Pope John Paul II on Violence. Hardcover, $21.95

The Rule of St. Benedict. "Remarkable for its discretion and its clarity," said St. Gregory the Great in 594 about the little book which had shaped his life, and stands today as one of the cornerstones of religious life. No rectory, no religious house, and no Catholic family should be without a copy of this seminal work. Hardcover, $16.95

The Scholar and the Cross, *Hilda C. Graef.* Life and work of Catholic convert Edith Stein who was killed by the Nazis. Great book for a Catholic reading group. Hardcover, $27.95

The Secret of Dreams, *Rev. Pedro Meseguer, S.J.* The only serious Catholic guide to understanding and interpreting dreams. Fr. Meseguer reveals the important role—strongly supported by tradition—that dreams can play in the Christian spiritual life, where they can be of the utmost use to confessors and penitents. Softcover, *$24.80*

Sins of Parents, *Fr. Charles Hugo Doyle.* Arresting guide to Catholic parenting, back in print after half a century. What are the mistakes parents make? How can you avoid them, or lessen their impact, if made? Hardcover, *$19.95*

Sex Psychology, *Rudolf Allers, M.D., Ph.D.* Landmark Catholic book on the psychology of sexuality by Sigmund Freud's most formidable opponent, Georgetown and Catholic University psychologist Rudolf Allers. Hardcover, *$28.95*

World's Great Catholic Literature. Anthology of Catholic literature, ideal for 12 to 18 year-olds or adults needing to brush up on their knowledge of the faith. **FREE Study Guide available to download on www.BooksforCatholics.com.** Hardcover, *$24.95*